THE GREAT EAST RIVER BRIDGE

THE GREAT EAST RIVER BRIDGE

1883 1983

The Brooklyn Museum

Exclusively distributed to the trade by
Harry N. Abrams, Inc., Publishers,
New York

Published for the exhibition
The Great East River Bridge
1883–1983
The Brooklyn Museum, New York
March 19–June 19, 1983

Cover:
Sigmund T. Meyers
American, b.1923
The Brooklyn Bridge 1976
(detail)
Dye transfer print
Collection: The artist

Frontispiece:
Joseph Stella
American, 1877–1946
American Landscape 1929
Oil on canvas
199.5 x 99.1 cm. (78½ x 39 in.)
Collection: Walker Art Center,
Minnesota

Designed and published by
The Brooklyn Museum, Division
of Publications and Marketing
Services, Eastern Parkway,
Brooklyn, New York 11238.
Printed in the USA by CLR, Inc.,
New York.

SPONSORED BY **THE CHASE MANHATTAN BANK**

Exclusively distributed to the
trade by
Harry N. Abrams, Inc.
Publishers
110 East 59th Street
New York, New York 10022

Library of Congress Cataloging in Publication Data
Main entry under title:

The Great East River Bridge, 1883-1983.

   Bibliography: p.
   1. Brooklyn Bridge (New York, N.Y.)
I. Brooklyn Museum.
TG25.N53G68   1983   624'.55'097471   83-2593
ISBN 0-8109-0982-0 (Abrams, hc)
ISBN 0-87273-096-4 (Brooklyn Museum, pbk.)

Contents

Anonymous
Fireworks off the Bridge *circa* 1883
Watercolor on paper
100.3 × 47.0 cm. (39½ × 18½ in.)
Collection: Municipal Archives of
the City of New York, inv. no. 150B

Drawn for the Unexcelled Fireworks
Company.

Preface

Willard C. Butcher
Chairman of the Board, The Chase Manhattan Bank

It is no surprise that the Brooklyn Bridge ranks high on everyone's list of wonders of the modern world. It is an immense, complex, and awesome structure. It is functional and beautiful. It has stood for one hundred years and links two boroughs of a great city—and the past with the present.

But the Brooklyn Bridge is also a symbol of the American spirit. The spirit that moved the project was the same that opened the West and built a great Industrial Revolution. This spirit was based on a firm belief in American technology, industry, and democracy.

Chase is proud to be a part of this centennial observance of the opening of the Brooklyn Bridge, because we believe that that spirit remains the key to our nation's future.

The hundred years since the Bridge's opening have seen an extraordinary growth in our country. As the original engineers could build a bridge to last one hundred years—to carry traffic of a kind and amount unthinkable in 1883—so can we, with the same kind of perseverance and dedication, prepare for a sound and prosperous nation one hundred years into the future.

The message of the Bridge is that it can be done, and Chase is delighted to bring that message to all the people of America on behalf of the people of New York.

Foreword

Michael Botwinick

Director, 1974-1982, The Brooklyn Museum

Linda S. Ferber

Acting Director, 1983, The Brooklyn Museum

There are few man-made structures that have so complete a hold on our imagination as the Brooklyn Bridge. Like the Eiffel Tower or the Empire State Building, it joins a select group of projects so strongly imprinted on our imagination that they step out of their eras and become timeless. Like the seven wonders of the ancient world, these modern achievements capture a very real glimmer of man's creative genius as a builder. They are constant reminders that architecture and engineering begin with the decision to address specific and practical needs but become more when the result is transcendent.

The Brooklyn Bridge moves beyond the essential problem of crossing a river and inhabits a loftier plane. It is in every way the symbol of its time. It expresses more completely than any painting one could think of the essence of that triumphant moment in the history of America when the combination of industry, science, democracy, and labor seemed able to dominate any problem. Encapsulating the history of New York in the last half of the nineteenth century, it speaks volumes about the Industrial Revolution, European immigration to America, entrepreneurs, Tammany politicians, and the recurrent American notion of taller, bigger, and better. Furthermore, it does all this with an unselfconscious splendor. That it is a scientific and political tour de force is one thing; that it remains, even today against a far more gigantic backdrop, an object of almost breathtaking beauty is quite another.

Undertaking an exhibition of the size and complexity of *The Great East River Bridge* requires the support and assistance of many people. Grateful acknowledgement goes to the lenders, without whose cooperation the exhibition would have been impossible. Likewise, we are grateful to the authors of the essays in this book: David McCullough, Steven Ross, Lewis Kachur, Dr. Albert Fein, and Deborah Nevins. Special thanks go to the staff of the Department of Paintings and Sculpture, particularly Assistant Curator Annette Blaugrund, who as coordinator of this exhibition worked miracles in bringing everything together; Assistant Curator Holly Connor, who helped to research the thousands of details connected with the exhibition; and Patricia Schwartz, whose unfailing patience and ability to organize those details were remarkable. We also thank Chief Designer Dan Weidmann, who did a brilliant job in designing the installation.

For extra time, helpfulness, and patience, we thank the following: Clark Beck (Rutgers University); Blair Birdsall (Steinman Boynton Gronquist & Birdsall); Commissioner Eugene J. Bockman (Department of Records and Information Services of the City of New York); Elizabeth Boone; Jennifer Bright and Steve Miller (Museum of the City of New York); Darlene Caruso, Anna Olsson, and Nadine Orenstein (Interns, Department of Painting and Sculpture, The Brooklyn Museum); Larry Casper (A.C.A. Gallery); Barbara Cohen (New York Bound Book Shop); Patricia Flavin (The Long Island Historical Society); Anne Gordon and Idillio Gracia Pena (Municipal Archives of the City of New York); Robert Gough and Tony Athling (Bureau of Highway Operations of the City of New York); Gail Guillette; Barbara Holloway (Engineering Society Library); Arthur Konop (St. Francis College); Paul Roebling; Richard Rudich; Wendy Shadwell and Helena Zinkham (The New-York Historical Society); Professor Gerald Silk (Columbia University); Elizabeth Campbell Stewart (Folsom Library, Rensselaer Polytechnic Institute); Robert Voegel (National Museum of American History); and Barbara Ward.

We are grateful to The Chase Manhattan Bank, whose leadership and commitment have assured that there would be a major recognition of the Brooklyn Bridge Centennial that has meaningful connections to people's lives.

We share in the pleasure and delight of everyone in reaching this moment of celebration. For years, Barbara Millstein, Curator of the Exhibition, has given of herself to remind us of the grandeur and spirit of this city. As Associate Curator of The Brooklyn Museum Sculpture Garden, she has labored, often literally in the shadows, to preserve a sense of our heritage. Few people have the passion and commitment necessary to bring off a project of this scope. To have attempted *The Great East River Bridge* without her energy and her knowledge and love of this city would have been folly.

1869—1883—1983

Deborah Nevins

Between 1869, when work on it began, and 1883, when it finally opened with celebrations unlike anything New Yorkers had ever seen, the Brooklyn Bridge remained constantly in the American consciousness. Lengthy articles about the Bridge's construction, the politics behind its financing, and the lives of its designers, John A. Roebling and his son Washington, appeared frequently in local, national, and even international journals and newspapers. As the Bridge took shape over the East River, it became a powerful presence in the everyday life of New Yorkers and a major attraction for tourists.

After its completion, the Bridge continued to capture the imagination of many as a manifestation of the power of civilization to conquer nature; its towers were among the tallest structures on the continent, and its span the longest in the world. As John Roebling had predicted, it became an inspiration to Americans and a national landmark.

The following images—most of which lie unknown, except to specialists, in the wonderful archives of New York's museums and libraries— convey some of the excitement and fascination that the Bridge has always created. These images provide an understanding of the context in which the Bridge was built, survey the Roeblings' engineering achievements, suggest what New York and Brooklyn looked like from the mid-nineteenth century through the time the Bridge was opened, and convey in brief a history of the way in which the Bridge has inspired countless artists and photographers.

The severe hardships engendered by the settlement and exploration of the American continent were often accompanied by an almost religious exultation at man's ability to subdue nature. Industrialization and remarkable technological advances in the nineteenth century, especially in the New World, suggested a hope and sense of mission which found realization in the spirit of "Manifest Destiny." This notion of the unity of the continent as divinely ordained was expressed well in Walt Whitman's 1871 poem "Passage to India," which hailed the movement of civilization to the Pacific coast and beyond. "Nature and Man shall be disjoin'd and diffused no more,"

Whitman wrote, "The true son of God shall absolutely fuse them." The actual physical joining of the East and West by bridge, canal, and railroad was thus more than metaphor; it was principle.

John Roebling believed in this principle. He saw the Brooklyn Bridge as an essential part of a continuous highway from East to West, and surveying for the Bridge was begun the same year (1869) that the transcontinental railroad was completed. Roebling's sense of mission led him to view the forms of suspension-bridge design and the goals of engineering in metaphysical terms: the curve of a bridge's cables was based on an elemental curve of nature, the catenary, and in the combination of tension and compression in his bridges Roebling saw the forces of nature in a state of idealized harmony.

In the 1872 painting *American Progress (Manifest Destiny)*, Roebling's bridge over the East River symbolizes the critical role of transportation and communication in the westward movement of civilization. As the sun rises over the Bridge and the railroad network spreading out to the West, the figure of "Progress" draws a telegraph wire behind her, and men advance with plow and wagon, driving the wild beasts and the Indians ahead of them. The only women are an Indian and "Progress" herself. Not a hint of failure, backsliding, or complexity intrudes into this tidy image.

John Gast
American
American Progress (Manifest Destiny) 1872
Oil on canvas
32.4 x 42.5 cm. (12¾ x 16¾ in.)
Collection: The Congoleum Collection, New Hampshire
Photo courtesy: Christie, Manson & Woods International, Inc., New York

John A. Roebling was one of the greatest minds of nineteenth-century America. Born in Germany in 1806, he studied engineering in Berlin and was both a student and a friend of the metaphysician Georg Wilhelm Friedrich Hegel. Attracted by the democracy and economic opportunities of America, he left Germany with his brother Karl in 1831 to seek land in the United States for a colonizing party to follow. On 1,600 acres of cheap land he bought in Butler County, Pennsylvania, twenty-five miles from Pittsburgh, he laid out a little village called Saxonburg. Here he tried his hand at farming and canary breeding, both unsuccessfully, before rededicating himself to engineering.

Canal transportation was of vital importance at the time, and Roebling worked as surveyor and engineer for numerous construction projects of the Pennsylvania canal system. The many mountain chains in the state were crossed by means of portage railways which carried barges and passenger cars up steep inclines using hemp rope and steam engines. The rope wore quickly and required frequent replacement. After an accident in which two men were killed when a rope failed, Roebling turned his attention to manufacturing rope from iron wire, remembering a description of such a cable in a German periodical. In 1841 he produced the first wire rope in America at his Saxonburg farm.

At Saxonburg, Roebling displayed the administrative abilities and ingenuity which were to be the hallmarks of his career. Using machines of his own design and the labor of his friends and neighbors, Roebling produced cables made from wire strands in which all the wires were evenly tensioned. The great strength and reliability of the new wire rope were soon proven in practice, and eventually all the Pennsylvania canals used the cables. Other applications were found in rigging, hoists, tow lines, and suspension structures.

Saxonburg, which became an industrial town, remained Roebling's home until 1849. Seeking access to the market and industrial centers further east, he then moved his home and expanding business to Trenton, New Jersey.

When John Roebling died in 1869 following an accident on the Brooklyn Bridge site, his son Washington A. Roebling assumed his responsibilities. Trained at Rensselaer Polytechnic Institute in Troy, New York, Washington had worked on his father's suspension bridges after graduation. Nonetheless, the building of the Brooklyn Bridge was an awesome task which drove him to exhaustion.

Washington Roebling believed that management should take as many risks as labor, and he continually went down into the Bridge's underwater foundations, or caissons, both in normal circumstances and in situations of

Anonymous photograph of
John A. Roebling (1806-1869),
aged 59
*Collection: Rutgers University,
New Jersey*

John Roebling's pass for the New York and Brooklyn Bridge
*Collection: Rutgers University,
New Jersey*

The Bridge was officially called the New York and Brooklyn Bridge until its name was changed to the Brooklyn Bridge in 1915—a change that seems just since Brooklyn paid for two-thirds of its cost. Over the last hundred years the Bridge has also been known as the Empire Bridge, the Great Bridge, the Roebling Bridge, and, of course, the Great East River Bridge.

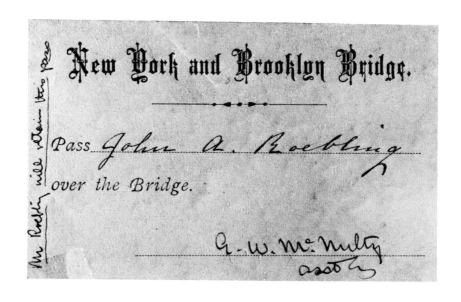

crisis. In 1871 he experienced the terrible effects of caisson disease, or the bends, and in 1872 his physical suffering combined with anxiety and fatigue turned him into a permanent invalid. Although he never went to the Bridge site again, he continued to direct the construction of the Bridge—first from his home in Trenton, New Jersey, and later from his house on Brooklyn Heights.

A woman of tremendous fortitude and intelligence, Emily Roebling was her husband Washington's chief aide in building the Bridge. She took Roebling's correspondence, read all important documents to him, communicated in person with the board of directors and the engineers, and provided Roebling eyewitness accounts of the construction progress. Without her energy and reliability, Washington Roebling could not have continued on the project after 1872.

Left: Anonymous photograph of **Washington A. Roebling** (1837–1926), *circa* 1870
Collection: Rutgers University, New Jersey

Right: Anonymous photograph of **Emily Warren Roebling** (1843–1903), *circa* 1880
Collection: Rutgers University, New Jersey

Below: **Washington A. Roebling in his sickroom**
Frank Leslie's Illustrated Newspaper, May 26, 1883

Right: Anonymous photograph of **Washington A. Roebling** *circa* 1895.
Collection: Rutgers University, New Jersey

The twenty-one years before John Roebling designed the Brooklyn Bridge were years in which he perfected in practice his understanding of the technology of suspension-bridge construction while building a series of aqueducts and bridges. By the time he faced the challenge of the Brooklyn project he was a master in his profession.

In 1822, when exploitation of the anthracite coalfields around the eastern Pennsylvania town of Lackawaxen began, river transport provided the sole means of moving this coal to the New York market and the sea. The Delaware and Hudson Canal Company was formed to build a canal that would permit barge traffic from the fields to the Hudson River. Beginning at Honesdale, Pennsylvania, the canal entered the Hudson at Roundout, New York. After the 108-mile-long waterway was fully opened in 1829, traffic increased rapidly from 7,000 to 192,000 tons by 1841. Despite modest enlargements, the canal and its locks soon proved inadequate.

In 1847, in order to alleviate the bottleneck in the system, Roebling designed two aqueducts to carry the canal over the Delaware and Lackawaxen Rivers. These aqueducts allowed canal barges to avoid the congestion of river traffic and the hazards of river ice. The aqueduct over the Delaware also removed the need to dam that river in order to create a pool over which the barges could travel.

With the construction in 1849-50 of two additional Roebling-designed aqueducts (one at Cuddelback, New York, over the Neversink River and one at High Falls, New York, over the Roundout Creek), the passage to New York City was cut by a full day. The canal competed successfully with the expanding railroad system until the 1870s, when railroads became the faster and more economical way to haul freight.

All four of Roebling's Delaware and Hudson aqueducts (and all of his subsequent bridges) were designed along the same lines as his Pittsburgh Aqueduct over the Allegheny River, built for the Pennsylvania State Canal in 1844-45. Unlike his competitor Charles Ellet, who left his cables bare, Roebling wrapped his cables with wire. These cables were attached to anchor bars which were in turn connected to anchor plates. Although this sort of anchorage was used in Europe at the time, Roebling improved it by imbedding the anchor plates in masonry and pouring cement grout over the anchor bars in order to provide protection against rust. Roebling also introduced the use of a timber grillage between anchor plate and masonry to distribute stress—a technique he patented in 1846.

The 535-foot-long Delaware Aqueduct was divided in four spans supported by masonry piers and carried by 8½-inch-diameter cables. Because the canal channel itself was constructed of timber arranged in a lattice truss able to carry the canal's own deadweight between the piers, the cables only had to support the weight of the water in the canal. Solid iron rods rather than wires were used to hang the canal deck from the spanning cables.

The Neversink Aqueduct at Cuddelback, New York, completed in 1850
Collection: The Delaware and Hudson Canal Historical Society, New York

When the canal system closed in 1898, the Delaware Aqueduct was easily converted to a highway bridge. The towpath for the draft animals was removed, and in the 1930s the bridge was redecked after a fire destroyed some of the original timber. The structure is now listed with the National Register of Historic Landmarks. It is considered the oldest suspension bridge in the world still completely intact.

The 170-foot-long single span of Roebling's aqueduct over the Neversink River was the longest of his Delaware and Hudson aqueducts. It was carried by 9½-inch-diameter cables, the largest ever made at the time. An analysis of the cables made in 1920 revealed no deterioration due to rust and no decline in the tensile strength of the cables' iron-wire strands. Unfortunately, today nothing remains of the abandoned structure but its masonry abutments.

The success of Roebling's Delaware and Hudson aqueducts greatly enhanced his prestige, and he was soon commissioned to design a bridge over the river at Niagara Falls. An international railway bridge over the Niagara gorge had first been suggested in 1845 by Major Charles Stuart, a civil engineer designing the route of Canada's Great Western Railway. The critical

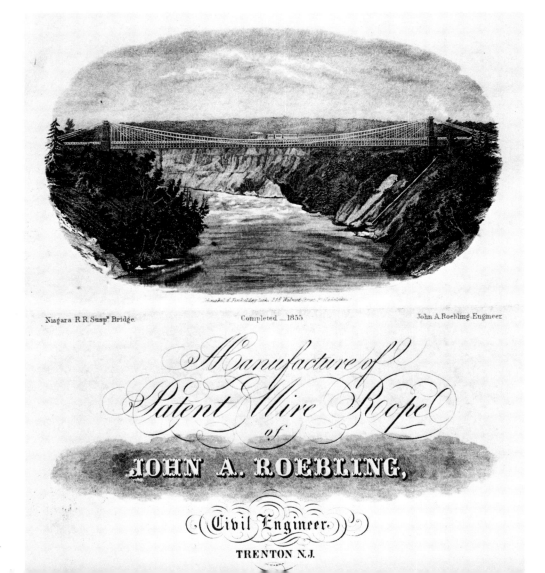

Niagara R.R. Suspⁿ Bridge   Completed — 1855   John A. Roebling Engineer

Manufacture of Patent Wire Rope of

JOHN A. ROEBLING,

Civil Engineer

TRENTON N.J.

Announcement by John A. Roebling's wireworks illustrating the Niagara Railway Suspension Bridge
Collection: Rutgers University, New Jersey

problem was how to support the dynamic load of a moving freight train. This was a very different problem than how to support the static load of an aqueduct, and Roebling's solution not only created the world's first wire-cable suspension bridge for railroads but also produced some critical analysis of the question of safety in all suspension structures.

Roebling had long advocated substantial stiffening of bridge roadbeds in order to resist all possible tempest and stress. The failure of Charles Ellet's suspension bridge over the Ohio River at Wheeling, West Virginia, in May 1854 confirmed his commitment to a system of trusses and inclined stays. After the Wheeling disaster, he added stays beneath the roadway of the Niagara Bridge in order to counter upward forces from the high winds frequently encountered at the site.

The bridge crossed the gorge in a single 825-foot span carried by four cables ten inches in diameter. Four masonry towers sixty feet high supported

the cables themselves. There were two levels: a 24-foot-wide upper deck for a single railway track, and a 15-foot-wide lower deck for carriages and pedestrian traffic. The arrangement of the cables—designed to carry six times their working load—was unique, with two attached to the lower deck, and two to the upper deck. Also unprecedented was the system of stiffening trusses, fully eighteen feet long, that occupied the entire depth between the two decks. Roebling was obliged to use timber for these trusses because iron was considered too costly.

The first fully loaded train crossed the gorge in March 1855, and the bridge remained in service until 1897. Eventually the timber trusses and the masonry towers were replaced with iron and steel ones—a change that required no interruption of train service. In its last years of service, as locomotives and freight cars increased in weight, the bridge carried loads three times its supposed capacity. Although the bridge has long since disappeared, the town adjacent to its United States abutment is still known as Suspension Bridge, New York.

In 1857 Roebling was commissioned to build a highway bridge over the Allegheny River at Pittsburgh to replace an antiquated and deteriorating

wooden-truss covered bridge. It was Roebling's third project in Pittsburgh, following the aqueduct for the Pennsylvania canal and a bridge over the Monongahela River that he completed in 1846. The Allegheny Bridge was made up of four spans totaling a length of 1,030 feet. For the first time Roebling used iron rather than timber for the suspended roadway structure, and wood was used only for the roadbed itself. The spans were supported by four cables spun in place, the principal cables requiring 4,200 trips of the wire spinning shuttle, and the outer smaller cables requiring 1,400 trips. Wrought-iron trusses ran the whole length of the bridge to stiffen the roadway, and inclined stays provided further rigidity. Six elegant iron towers supporting the cables rested on three massive granite piers that were rounded to deflect ice and current. This was the first of Roebling's bridges to be generously financed, suggesting the high confidence that investors placed in Roebling's now proven genius. Although the bridge was considered so sound and fire resistant that no insurance was carried on it, an 1881 fire caused by cinders from steamboats severely damaged the roadbed, necessitating its replacement. The bridge was demolished in 1891 and replaced by a larger structure. The construction of the Allegheny Bridge, initially directed by John Roebling, was eventually supervised by his son Washington, who joined his father in 1858 at the age of twenty-one.

Roebling also involved his son in the building of his bridge over the Ohio River between Cincinnati, Ohio, and Covington, Kentucky. Such a bridge had been envisioned by the citizens of Ohio and Kentucky since the early

The Cincinnati-Covington Bridge over the Ohio River, completed in 1867

nineteenth century, but the heavy river traffic which developed precluded any bridge that would impede passage by blocking the river with piers or by restricting the height of steam vessels. In an exhaustive analysis of 1846 Roebling refuted the arguments of the bridge opponents and assured the public of his command of the technology required. His confidence and experience allowed him to write: "The construction of suspension bridges is now so well understood that no competent builder will hesitate to resort to spans of 1,500 feet and more."

Investment in the bridge company languished, however, until 1856, when an energetic and devoted bridge enthusiast was elected to the board. Soon Roebling was ready to begin work. Masonry towers 230 feet tall were built near each shore on top of great timber platforms that were sunk under the water line to keep their wood from ever drying out and deteriorating. Cables 12½-inches in diameter were strung out over the towers and anchored in abutments on each side of the river. The financial panic of 1857 and the Civil War interrupted construction from 1858 to 1863, but the work continued after the war with Washington Roebling, discharged from the Army, assisting his father.

The Cincinnati-Covington Bridge, still in use, has a span between the towers of 1,057 feet, which made it the longest in the world when it was completed in 1867. Wrought-iron beams are the cross members on which an oak and pine deck was originally built. Two wrought-iron trusses run the whole length of the bridge's side, and Roebling's use of diagonal stays increases the stiffness of the bridge appreciably. These stays, running crosswise to the vertical suspender cables, were a Roebling innovation. Roebling wrote that "their sole office is to counteract any undulations which might be imparted to the cables in a severe gale." It was this precise understanding of the requirements of bridge engineering and its meticulous application which assured the success of all the suspension structures Roebling designed.

The Great Suspension Bridges of the United States
Scientific American, May 31, 1870
Courtesy: Rensselaer Polytechnic Institute Archives, New York

NIAGARA SUSPENSION BRIDGE

EAST RIVER SUSPENSION BRIDGE

Brooklyn's important daily, began publication in 1841 as a Democratic campaign paper, and Walt Whitman was its editor from 1846 to 1848. The Academy of Music was built in 1861, and The Long Island Historical Society was established in 1863. Fulton Street was the commercial center of the city.

Before the building of the Brooklyn Bridge, ferries provided the essential link between Brooklyn and New York. In 1860, 32 million passengers used the East River ferries; by 1868 the number was more than 50 million. Thirteen ferry boats completed more than one thousand crossings each day.

    Severe winters often made ferry crossings impossible, and the especially bitter winter of 1866-67 was important in persuading many influential Brooklynites that a bridge to New York was essential. That December, Roebling's Cincinnati bridge had opened with great success, confirming his abilities and insuring his choice as the designer of the bridge over the East River. Winning the contract was the fulfillment of Roebling's career and the realization of his ideas of the 1850s.

    Roebling himself had become obsessed with the idea of a bridge to Brooklyn after being icebound on a ferry in 1852. In 1856 he proposed a bridge over Blackwells Island (now Welfare Island); later he suggested a site nearer the present location. Although he submitted plans to the press in 1857 and 1860, the financial panic of 1857 and the Civil War delayed serious consideration of his proposal. Not until 1865 was a bridge company formed to seek support for construction and financing.

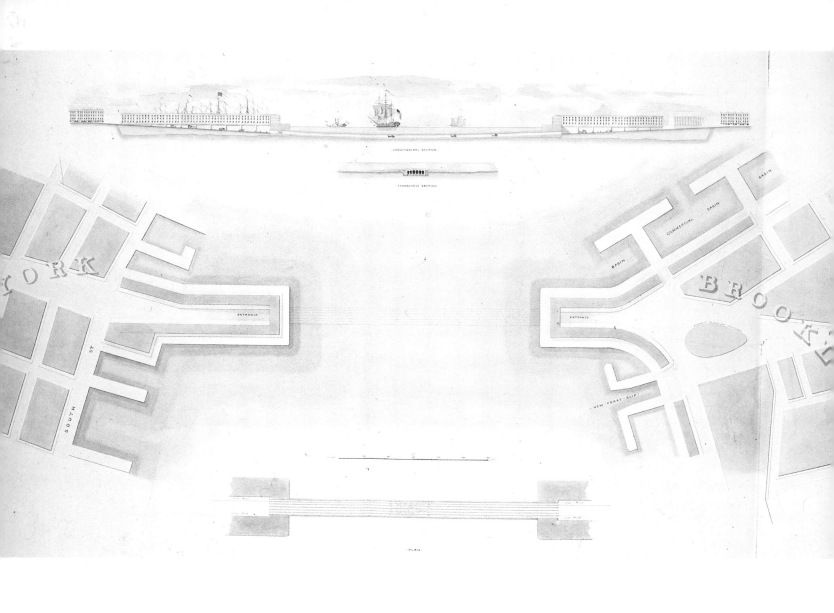

LONGITUDINAL SECTION

TRANSVERSE SECTION

YORK

SOUTH ST

ENTRANCE

BROOKLYN

BASIN   COMMERCIAL   BASIN   BASIN

ENTRANCE

NEW FERRY SLIP

PLAN

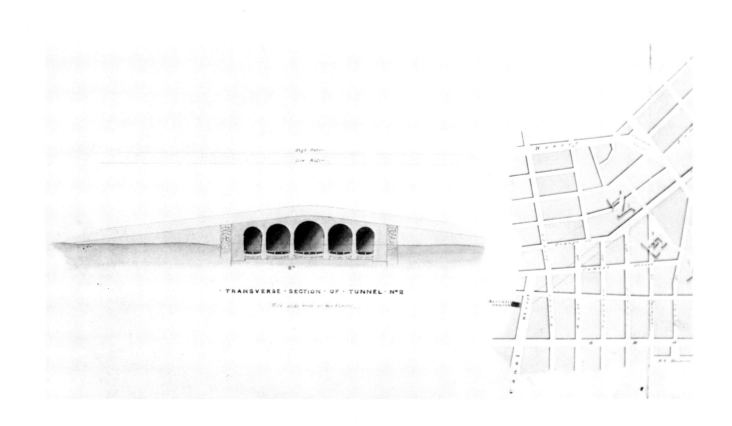

High Water

Low Water

TRANSVERSE · SECTION · OF · TUNNEL · Nº 2

In 1969, Francis Valentine, an engineer for
the New York City Department of Transportation, was sent to the department's carpentry shop under the Brooklyn end of the
Williamsburg Bridge to locate an engineering drawing needed for the repair of a small
element of the Brooklyn Bridge. To his
astonishment he found that the shop contained — in a state of complete disarray —
some ten thousand of the Bridge's original
blueprints and drawings, including many
by the Bridge's chief engineers John and
Washington Roebling.

It took Valentine four years to find someone who appreciated the documents' significance. When he did, it was someone he
played softball with, David Hupert, then
with the Whitney Museum of American
Art. In May 1976, Hupert mounted sixty-
five of the drawings in the Whitney's downtown gallery, and the exhibition was
extremely well received by the public. Eventually the drawings found a home at the
Municipal Archives of the City of New
York, and Barbara Millstein of The Brooklyn
Museum catalogued them. They are now
available for study on microfilm.

The great attention to detail and the
extensive use of color in these drawings

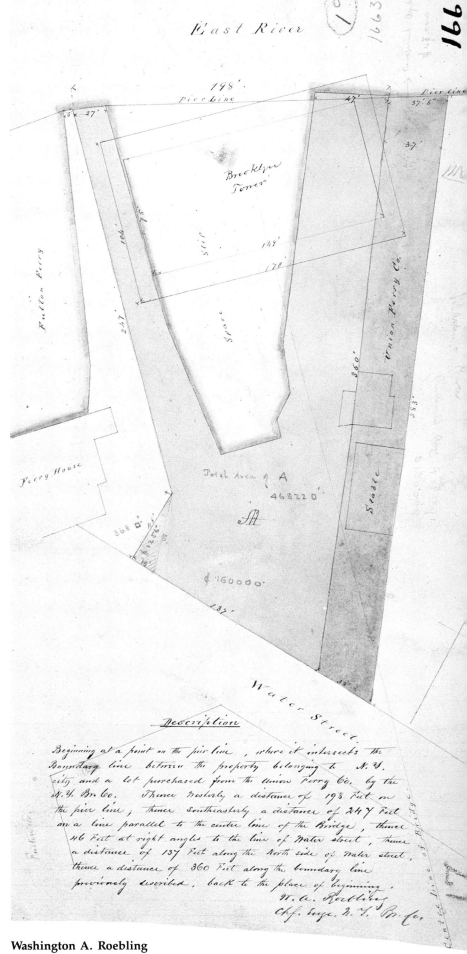

Washington A. Roebling
Property Map, Brooklyn Tower
circa 1867
Black ink, colored ink, and wash
on paper
38.7 x 19.7 cm. (15¼ x 17¾ in.),
irregular
*Collection: Municipal Archives of the
City of New York, inv. no. 783*

23

William Vanderbosch
Borings for the
Foundation of the
Brooklyn Tower 1869
Black ink, colored ink,
and watercolor on
paper
88.9 x 44.4 cm. (35 x
17½ in.)
Collection: Municipal
Archives of the City of
New York, inv. no. 2028
Photo courtesy: American
Heritage

Borings for the tower
foundations (right and
facing page) revealed
that a solid footing
would be closer to the
surface on the
Brooklyn side than on
the New York side,
meaning the New York
foundation would have
to be placed at a
greater depth.
Washington Roebling
was forced to
reexamine this original
plan, however, when
three men experienced
painful deaths due to
caisson disease during
the foundation
excavation on the New
York side. He decided
to settle the New York
tower on a compact,
extremely dense
foundation of gravel
and sand instead of
going deeper to find
bedrock.

24

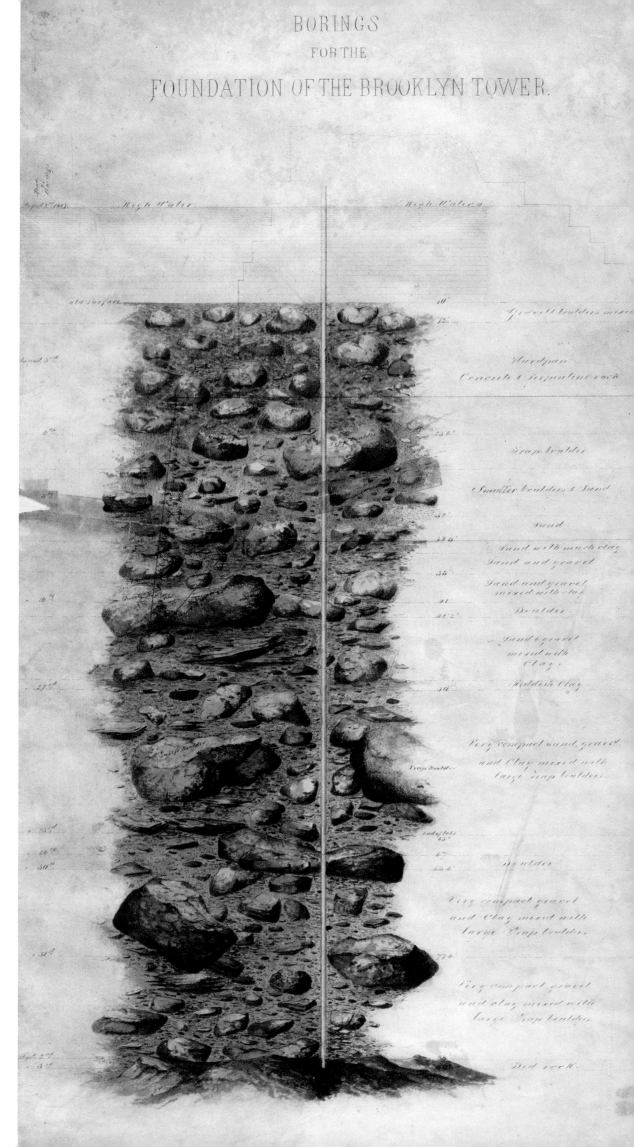

allow us to experience the Bridge in a way that we never can when we see the structure itself. In some instances, as in a rendering of the boring for the foundation of the Brooklyn tower (see page 24 opposite), the drawings have an almost photographic quality; in others, such as a depiction of men using a timber hoist (see gatefold, page 34), they are highly narrative. Still other drawings show us schemes for parts of the Bridge which were never built, giving us access to the thought processes of the Bridge's engineers.

The Brooklyn Bridge drawings are among the most extensive records of any nineteenth-century bridge in the United States. Their quality and number, and the fact that they document one of the most remarkable engineering achievements of all time, make them a national treasure.

William Vanderbosch
Borings for the Foundation of the New York Tower n.d.
Black ink, colored ink, and watercolor on paper
82.8 x 38.1 cm. (32¼ x 15 in.)
Collection: Municipal Archives of the City of New York, inv. no. 5893

BORINGS
FOR THE
FOUNDATION OF THE N.Y. TOWER.

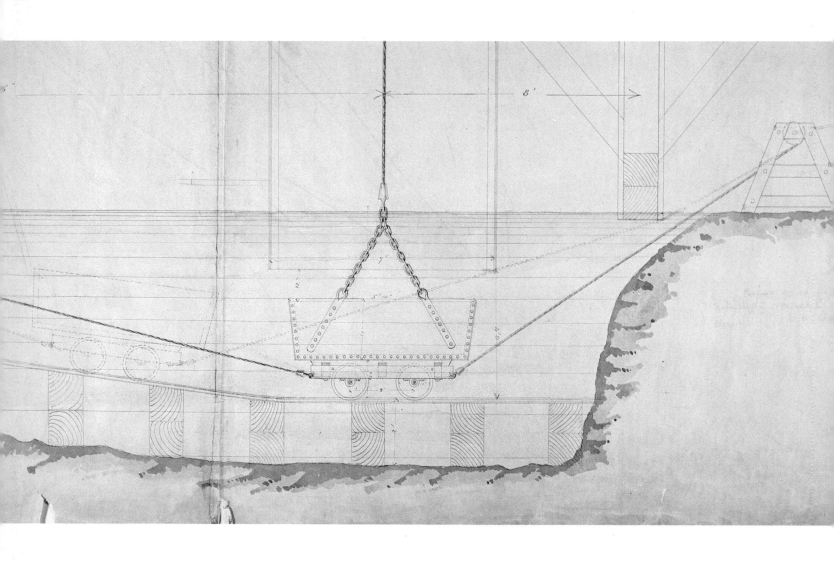

**Washington A. Roebling
Hoisting Pan System for Debris
Removal (Brooklyn Caisson)**
October 1870
Black ink and colored ink on
paper
59.0 x 62.2 cm. (23¼ x 24½ in.)
*Collection: Municipal Archives of the
City of New York, inv. no. 644*

Each of the Brooklyn Bridge's towers was built on top of a giant watertight chamber called a pneumatic caisson. A hollow wooden box with V-shaped sides and a solid roof of interlocking courses of timber, the caisson was partially constructed on land and then launched into the river (see pages 30-31). After launching, additional courses were added to the roof, and the first courses of stone for the tower were laid, depressing the caisson to the riverbed. Compressed air was then pumped into the chamber, prohibiting the entry of water. Men entered the chamber through air locks and began excavating the riverbed. As the digging went on below, the tower was simultaneously constructed above, forcing the caisson ever deeper (see illustration on facing page, bottom). When the caisson reached ground firm enough to support the entire weight of the tower, it was filled with concrete.

The material that was excavated from the riverbed had to be removed from the caisson, and the engineers designed at least three methods for doing so. All involved the use of a water shaft that was to extend into a pool deeper than the caisson itself. In the system depicted above, a cart was to be lowered down the shaft, pulled to one side of the pool, filled, and then lifted up the shaft. In the scheme shown on the facing page, a chamber was to be lowered from above, filled with debris dumped down two side chutes, and then hoisted to the top. Finally, in the system that was actually used (see gatefold, page 33), a "clamshell" scoop dropped down the shaft and, in an action Washington Roebling likened to that of a person picking up a handful of stones, grabbed the material the workers had deposited in the pool and brought it to the surface.

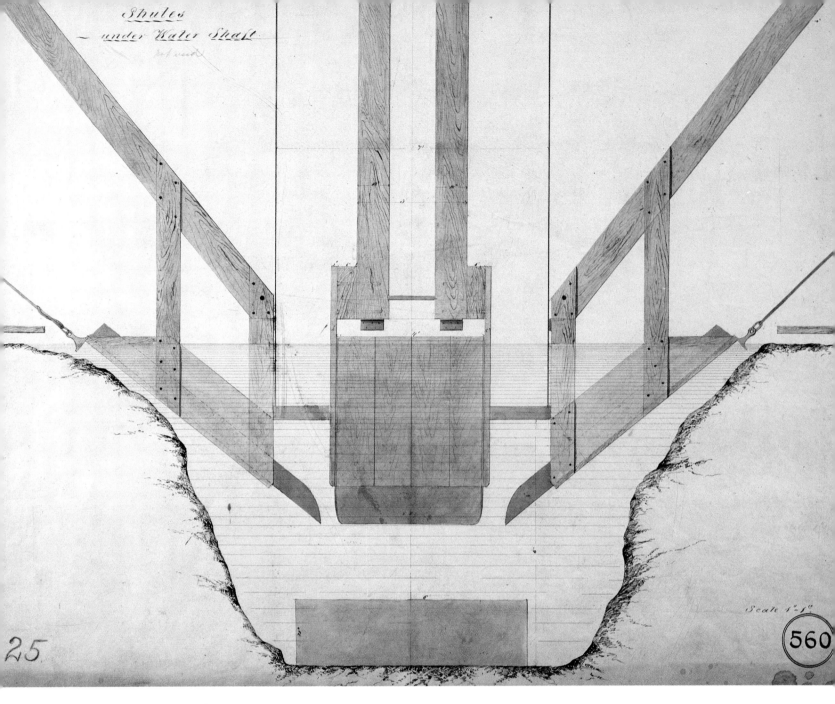

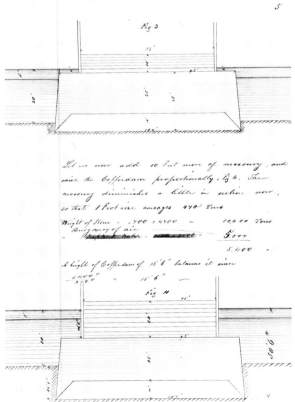

Above:
Anonymous
Chutes under Water Shaft for
Brooklyn Caisson (unrealized)
circa 1869
Black ink and colored ink on
paper
48.2 x 59.7 cm. (19 x 23½ in.)
Collection: Municipal Archives of the
City of New York, inv. no. 647
Photo courtesy: American Heritage

Left:
John A. Roebling
Study and Calculations
Demonstrating the Sinking of the
Caisson as Continuous Layers of
Stone are Laid n.d.
Black ink and red ink on paper
32.4 x 20.3 cm. (12¾ x 8 in.)
Collection: Rensselear Polytechnic
Institute Archives, New York

Washington A. Roebling
Placement of Hardware in Timber
in Second Course of Brooklyn
Caisson n.d.
Pencil, black ink, colored ink, and
watercolor on paper
47.6 x 59.0 cm. (18¾ x 23¼ in.)
Collection: Municipal Archives of the
City of New York, inv. no. 608

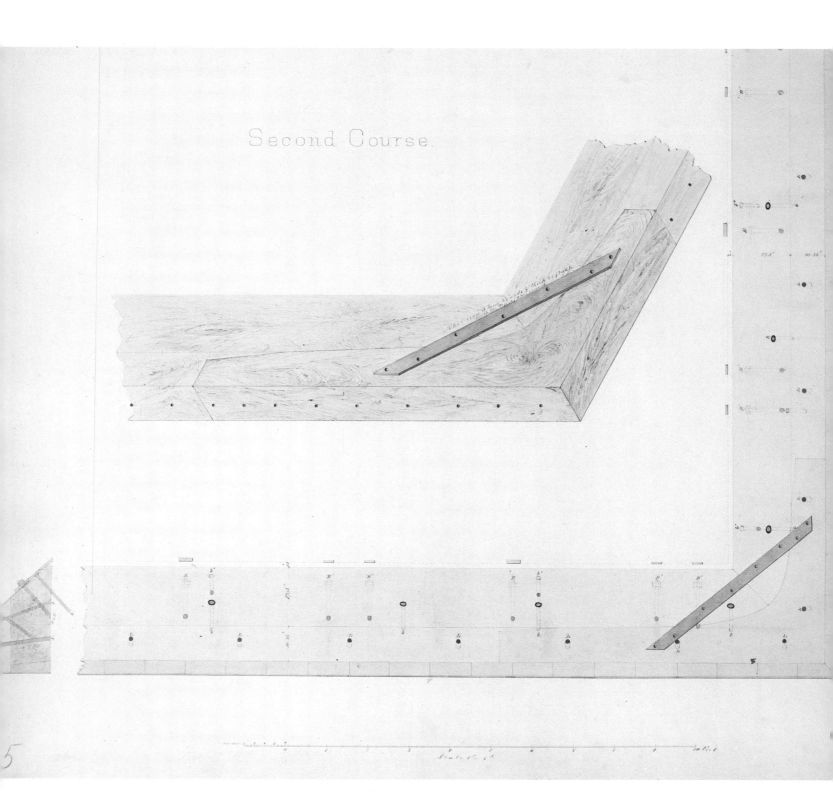

Washington A. Roebling
Section through the Long Side of
the Brooklyn Caisson Showing
Arrangement of Bolts n.d.
Black ink, colored ink, and
watercolor on paper
45.7 x 59.3 cm. (18 x 23⅜ in.)
Collection: Municipal Archives of the
City of New York, inv. no. 655

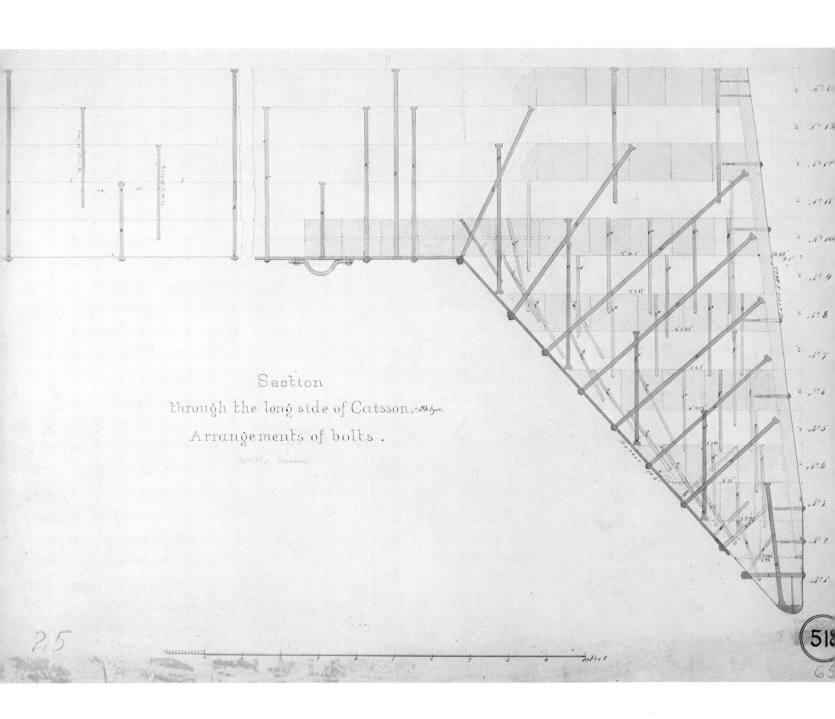

Section

through the long side of Caisson.=Bklyn.

Arrangements of bolts.

29

The Brooklyn caisson before launching March 1870
Collection: Museum of the City of New York

The Brooklyn Bridge was not the first bridge to be built on pneumatic caissons. Caissons had been invented in Europe (where Washington Roebling had studied them on a trip with his wife), and they had first been used in the United States in 1864 on a bridge at St. Louis designed by James Eads. Still, the Brooklyn Bridge's caissons were the largest the world had ever seen.

The caisson for the Brooklyn side of the river weighed 3,000 tons and measured 168 by 102 feet—half a city block. It was built four miles upriver from its final resting place in a drydock about a hundred feet from the shore. On March 19, 1870, it was launched into the river (see illustration facing page, bottom), and on May 3 it was towed by tugs to a spot by the Fulton Ferry. There, the following day, it was maneuvered or "warped" into place in a three-sided basin that had been dredged out of the river (see illustration facing page, top).

Dredging this basin had proved difficult. The riverbed was so strewn with boulders that the material had to be blasted out during the night (so as not to disrupt the ferry) and dredged by day. After more than a month of blasting (with an average of thirty-five blasts a night) hardly a dent had been made. The original plan to dredge the entire basin to a depth of eighteen feet at high tide was abandoned, and only the edges of the basin were dug before the caisson was warped into place. In this, as in several other instances during the long years of building the Bridge, Washington Roebling and his engineers had to make quick and difficult decisions in the face of unforeseen circumstances.

Once in position, the Brooklyn caisson was built even bigger. Having measured 14 feet 6 inches high at launching (with a roof five feet thick), it grew seven feet taller as additional timber courses were laid on.

A number of measures were taken to insure that the caisson would remain airtight as it sunk into the riverbed. The seams were caulked with oakum, a rope permeated with tar; a special airtight varnish was applied to the timbers; the lower three feet of the caisson, inside and out, were clad in boiler plate; hot pitch was poured between all the courses of the roof; and a tin sheath was laid between the fourth and fifth courses and wrapped around the perimeter.

As mighty a structure as it was, the Brooklyn caisson would soon be surpassed by its New York counterpart. That caisson would be ten feet taller at completion.

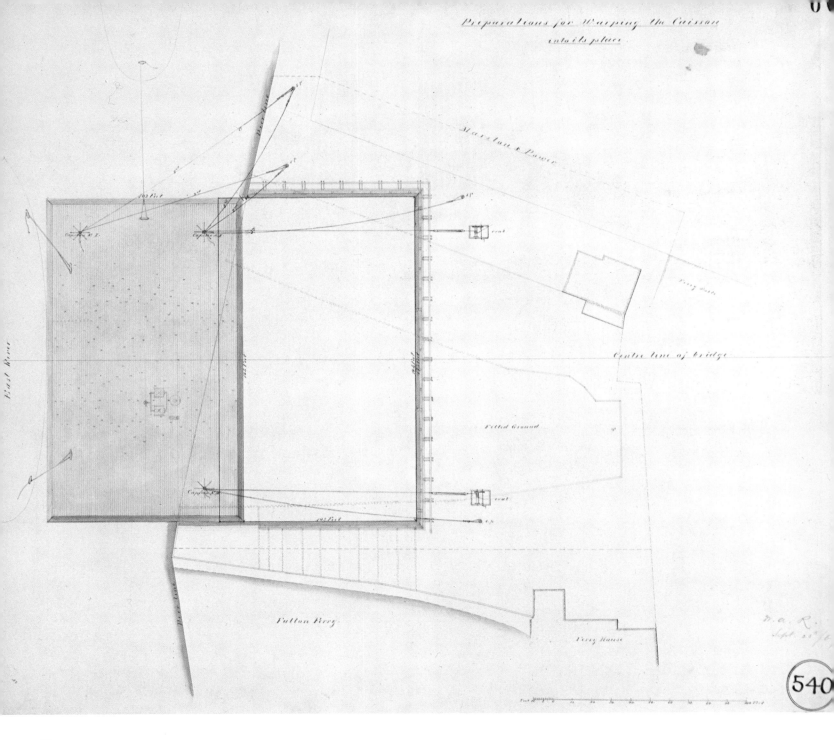

Above:
Washington A. Roebling
Site and Preparations for Warping
of Brooklyn Caisson into Place
September 28, 1869
Black ink, colored ink, pencil, and
watercolor on paper
49.5 x 76.8 cm. (19½ x 30¼ in.)
Collection: Municipal Archives of the
City of New York, inv. no. 653

Below:
Launching of the Brooklyn
caisson *The Technologist, 1870*
Collection: Rensselaear Polytechnic
Institute Archives, New York

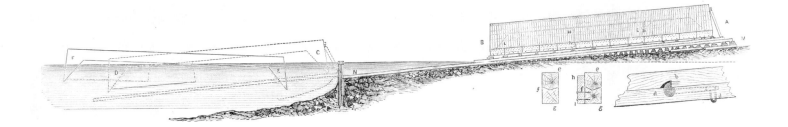

Water-Shaft   32' 3"   Entrance-Shaft

20' 6"   1' 4"   33' 6"   8' 6"

27' 6"

21' 3"

10' 3"   33"

26

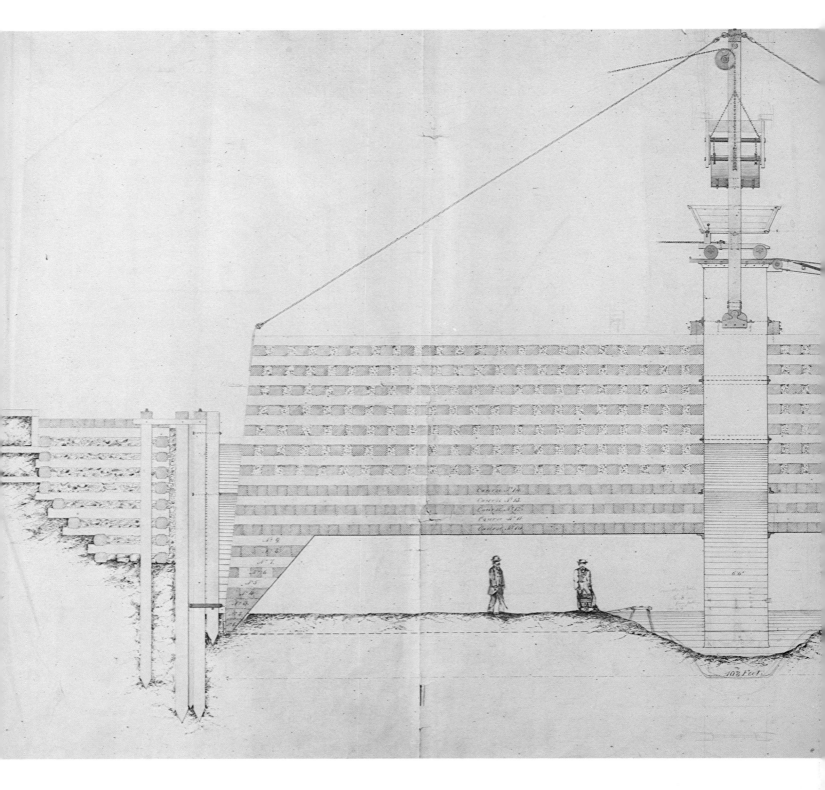

The Brooklyn caisson was divided into six working chambers. At first digging was done entirely by hand. But it soon became apparent that this would take too long, and explosives were also used. This difficult work took place in an environment which was abominable. The men had to contend not only with heat, tremendous humidity, and an awful stench but also with the dreaded caisson disease, which science was just beginning to understand in the 1870s.

Washington A. Roebling
Caisson in Position,
Brooklyn Side
September 28, 1869
Black ink, colored ink, pencil, and watercolor on paper
49.2 x 121.3 cm. (19⅜ x 47¾ in.)
Collection: Municipal Archives of the City of New York, inv. no. 656

Facing page:
Washington A. Roebling
Longitudinal Section of New York
Caisson (*detail*) 1869
Black ink and colored ink on paper
Collection: Municipal Archives of the City of New York, inv. no. 4307
Photo courtesy: American Heritage

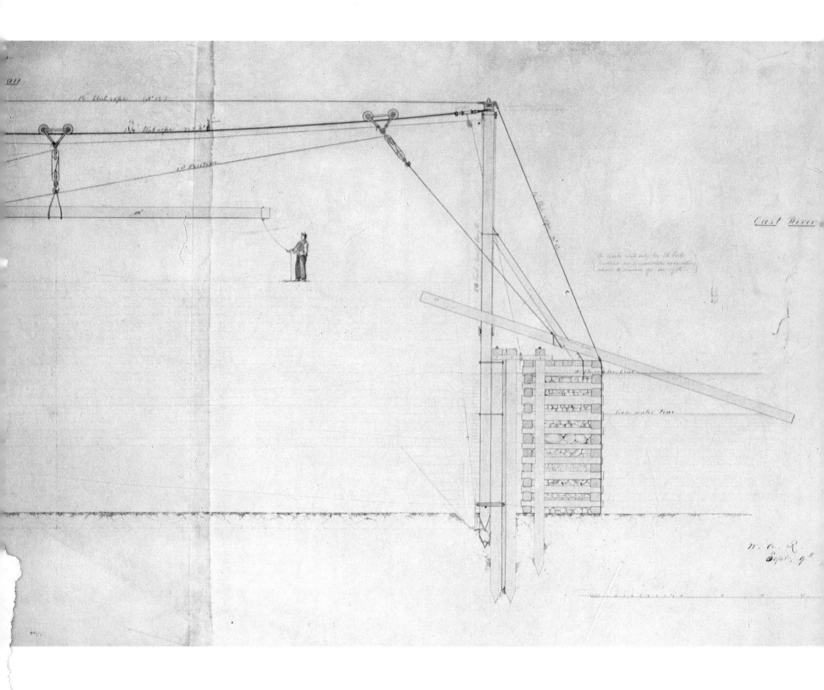

Washington A. Roebling
Brooklyn Caisson, Timber Hoist
September 9, 1869
Black ink and colored ink on
paper
49.5 x 160.6 cm. (19½ x 63¼ in.)
Collection: Municipal Archives of the
City of New York, inv. no. 648
Photo courtesy: American Heritage

Washington Roebling knew that he would have to dig deeper on the New York side to reach a solid foundation. This would require a longer period of excavation and a longer underwater section of the stone tower. Roebling therefore modified the design of the New York caisson (see facing page) to meet the challenge of a situation even more hazardous than that on the Brooklyn side. The caisson itself was larger, measuring 102 by 172 feet, with seven more courses of timber. Each air lock had a capacity for sixty men instead of the twelve man capacity of the air locks in the Brooklyn caisson. Thirteen air compressors were used instead of six. The caisson was now entirely sheathed in iron boiler plate to protect against fire, and the inside walls were whitewashed to reflect more light. Fifty sand-removal pipes each four inches in diameter extended to one foot above the working surface. As the top of a tube was opened from above, the compressed air of the chamber forced sand and small debris out. The New York caisson was sunk thirty-four feet deeper than the Brooklyn one. In the Brooklyn caisson, communication between the workers below and the men above had often been difficult; for the New York caisson an inventive mechanical communication system was developed. It used maps and indicators and short messages on boards channeled through a pipe.

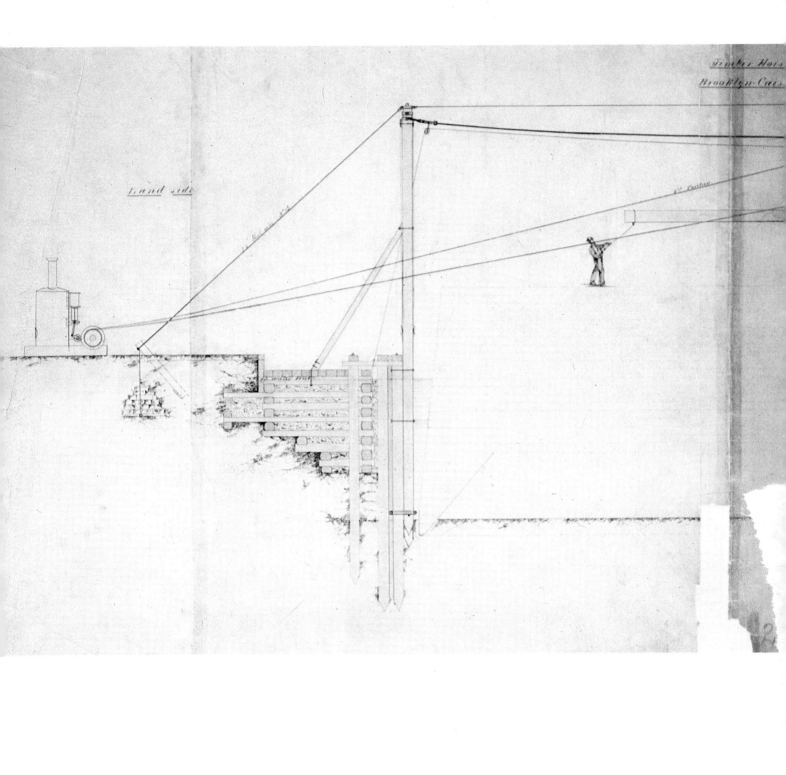

Wilhelm Hildenbrand
American, *circa* 1845-1908
**New York Caisson, Transverse
Section through the Air Locks** n.d.
Black ink and colored ink on
paper
66.0 x 88.4 cm. (26 x 33¼ in.)
*Collection: Municipal Archives of the
City of New York, inv. no. 4309*
Photo courtesy: American Heritage

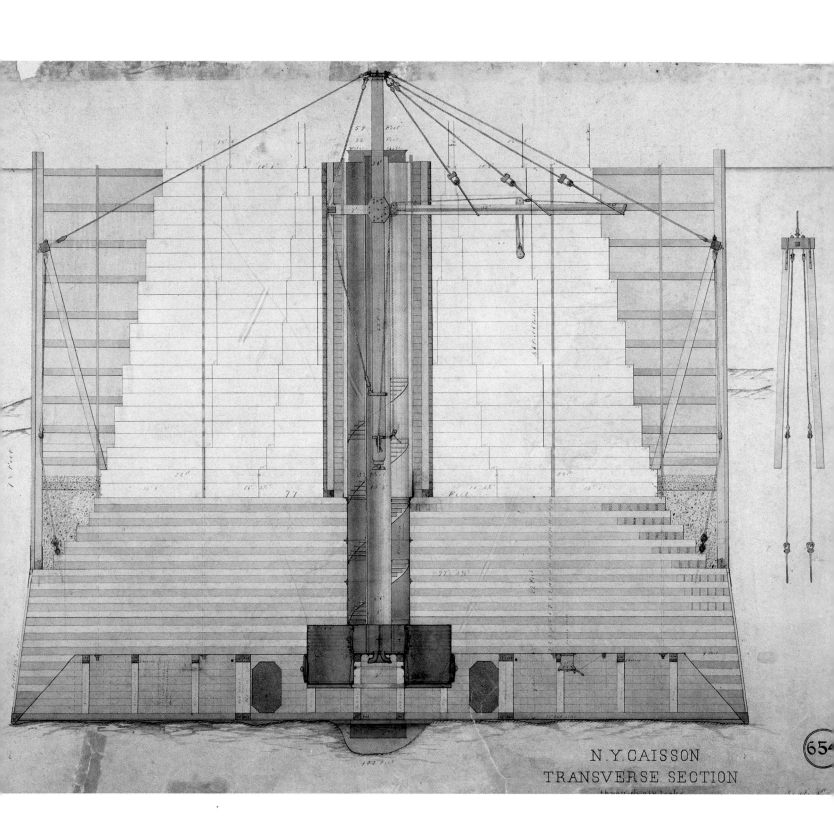

N.Y. CAISSON
TRANSVERSE SECTION

65

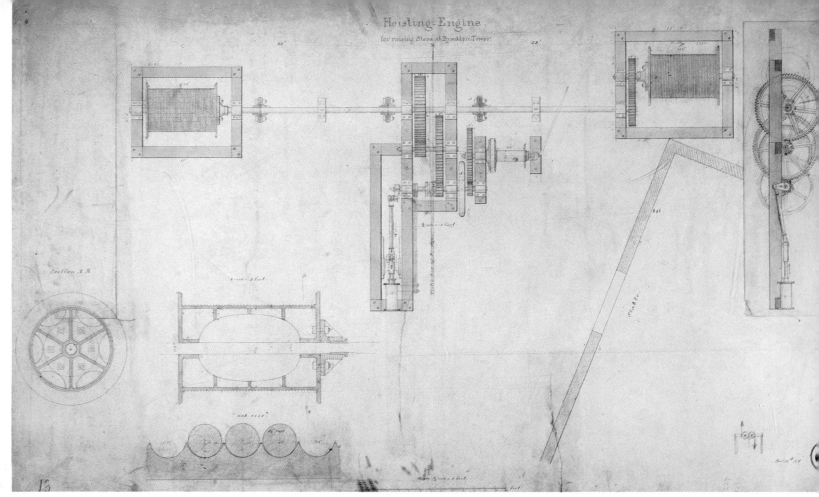

Above:
Washington A. Roebling and
Wilhelm Hildenbrand
Hoisting Engine for Raising
Stone, Brooklyn Tower
April 16, 1871
Black ink, brown ink, and pencil
on paper
62.8 x 98.4 cm. (24¾ x 38¾ in.)
Collection: Municipal Archives of the
City of New York, inv. no. 2048
Photo courtesy: American Heritage

Below:
Silas A. Holmes
New York Tower, 39th Course of
Masonry Complete
September 21, 1872
Collection: Museum of the City of
New York

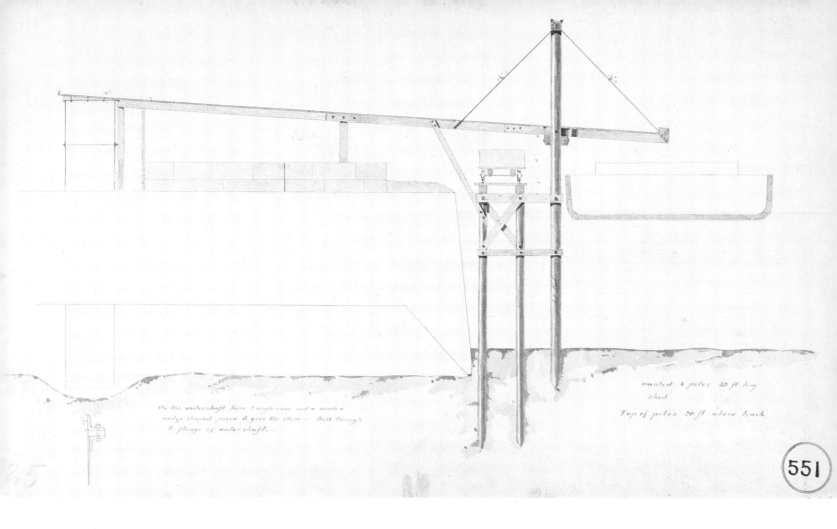

The Bridge's towers consisted of New York limestone below the high water mark and Maine granite above. The blocks were transported by schooner to Red Hook, Brooklyn, and then hauled to the tower on scows. Boom derricks hoisted the stones until the tower became too tall for the derricks to do the work. Then a system of pulleys run by steam was used. The stones were attached to a hook on the pulley by means of iron eyebolts attached to the blocks. At the top of the tower the blocks were placed on flat cars and moved near their final location. A boom derrick then placed them in their exact places in the stone course.

An average of twenty blocks an hour were laid, and construction was continuous except for the winter months. When complete, the New York tower contained 46,945 cubic yards of stone, and the Brooklyn tower 38,214.

Washington A. Roebling
Railroad Track from Brooklyn Caisson to Scow with Instructions for Putting a Wooden Wedge below Track to Provide Slope
circa 1870
Black ink, colored ink, and watercolor on paper
48.9 x 61.3 cm. (19¼ x 24⅛ in.)
Collection: Municipal Archives of the City of New York, inv. no. 646

This drawing shows the short span of elevated railroad track that was used to transport stones from scows to the tower.

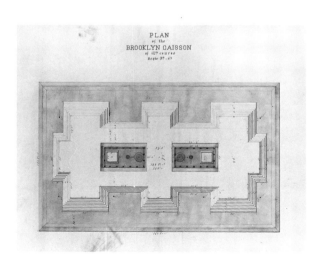

Washington A. Roebling
Plan of the Brooklyn Caisson
August 29, 1869
Black ink, colored ink, and watercolor on paper
49.5 x 61.0 cm (19½ x 24 in.)
Collection: Municipal Archives of the City of New York, inv. no. 654

Wilhelm Hildenbrand and
Washington A. Roebling
**New York Tower of the Brooklyn
Bridge** April 23, 1873
Pencil, black ink, and colored ink
on paper
100.6 x 55.5 cm. (39⅝ x 21⅞ in.)
*Collection: Municipal Archives of the
City of New York, inv. no. 7813*
Photo courtesy: American Heritage

In this drawing of the New York
tower, Wilhelm Hildenbrand and
Washington Roebling imagined
how the tower would interact with
the environment. Every stone is
rendered in light and shade—thus
dramatizing each block's physical
qualities—and the tower's reflection
in the river is subtly drawn.

Left:
Silas A. Holmes
The Brooklyn Tower September 1872
*Collection: Museum of the City of
New York*

On June l5, 1870, three months
after the launching of the Brooklyn
caisson, the first stone of the
Brooklyn tower was laid. By June
1872, three months before this
photograph was taken, the tower
had risen a hundred feet above the
high water mark; three years later,
at completion, it was 178 feet taller.
At the high water mark the tower
measured 140 by 59 feet.

Below:
Talfor
New York Caisson 1871
*Collection: Museum of the City of
New York*

E. Frank Farrington, the Bridge's
master mechanic, wrote about
work in the New York caisson:
"What with the flaming lights, the
deep shadows, the confusing
noises of hammers, drills and
chains, the half naked forms
flitting about, with here and there
a sysaphus rolling his stone, one
might, if of a poetic temperament,
get a realizing sense of Dante's
Inferno!"

Brooklyn tower near completion
circa 1875
Collection: Museum of the City of New York

In his 1881 *Concise Description of the East River Bridge with Full Details of the Construction*, E. Frank Farrington told of being on top of the Brooklyn tower while it was being built.

"It was in the early morning," Farrington wrote, "when a dense fog covered the whole region, that having occasion to examine some machinery, I went on the tower before the time for commencing work. I shall never forget that morning. I found the fog had risen to within twenty feet of the top of the tower, and there it hung dense, opaque, tangible. It was what you might seem to cut with a knife. It seemed that I might jump down and walk upon it unharmed. It looked like a dull ocean of lead-colored little billows; vast, dead, immovable . . . . The spires of Trinity in New York, and in Brooklyn, and the tops of the masts of a ship in one of the dry docks, with the roof of the bridge towers, were all that were visible of the world below."

Silas A. Holmes
New York Caisson
March 1872
Collection: Museum of the City of New York

The New York caisson was launched May 8, 1871. By October 31, when the first stone for the New York tower was laid, the Brooklyn tower was already well above the water. In this image the first courses of stone above the New York caisson are visible. In the photographs on the following three pages the progress of the New York tower's construction can be watched as stone by stone it rises to completion over four years.

Above, left:
Silas A. Holmes
New York Tower, Construction
Pier
March 1872
Collection: Museum of the City of
New York

The New York tower's 300-foot-
long construction pier supported
buildings for machinery and
materials. The scows docked
alongside the pier are loaded with
stone blocks for the tower. The
Brooklyn tower and the Fulton
Ferry slip are visible in the
background.

Above:
Silas A. Holmes
New York Tower, Thirty-ninth
Course of Masonry Complete
September 19, 1872
Collection: Museum of the City of
New York

Left:
New York tower
September 1873
Collection: Museum of the City of
New York

**New York tower from the
Brooklyn side, 1875**
*Collection: Museum of the City of
New York*

42

Joshua H. Beals
Section of Panorama of New York Taken from the Brooklyn Tower
1875-76
Collection: The New-York Historical Society

This extraordinary photograph taken from the top of the Brooklyn tower is part of a composite panorama of Manhattan. The huge low building to the left of the New York tower is the post office designed by Alfred Mullet. The building with the spire to the right of the post office is the Tribune Building designed by Richard Morris Hunt.

Bridge towers viewed from New York
July 1876
Collection: Museum of the City of New York

With the towers well underway, the anchorage and approach structures were begun—in Brooklyn in February 1873 and in New York in May 1875. In this image the New York anchorage is under construction amidst the dense fabric of Manhattan's buildings.

"Probably to the end of time", *Harper's* magazine wrote in 1883, "thoughtful spectators unversed in the mysteries of engineering will pause, as they now do, before these gigantic towers, more wonderful than the Pyramids, with the everlasting sea beating their mighty bases, and will perplex themselves in vain to imagine by what means the granite masonry could have been laid so solid and true beneath not forty feet depth of rushing tides alone, but eighty feet below their surface, on the rock which those tides had not touched for untold ages."

Frank Leslie's Illustrated Newspaper
July 5, 1873
Collection: Private Collection, New York

Until New York's infamous Tweed Ring was destroyed in 1871, its leaders profited from the Bridge by manipulating the construction funds and insuring jobs and contracts for their friends. The two men depicted in this editorial cartoon, William Kingsley and William Fowler, had ties to the Ring.

William Kingsley, a Brooklyn contractor, was a major force in the organization of the Bridge Company and became the General Superintendent of the Bridge. William Fowler, a member of the Brooklyn Board of Public Works,

was powerful in the Brooklyn Democratic machine. Republicans described him as the "good-natured, round cheeked, jolliest of robbers whose rollicking way of making his steals have (sic) cost the public millions . . ."

The article which accompanied the cartoon was full of innuendos to the effect that these men were making money off the Bridge. It was substantiated that at least Kingsley did.

Anchor plate
Scientific American,
January 8, 1876
Courtesy: Columbia University, New York

The work on the Bridge was organized so that both the anchorage structures and the towers would be completed at once. Only when the anchorages were complete, ready to secure the cables and resist their tremendous pull, could cable spinning begin. The anchorage system John Roebling had devised in his earlier bridges was used here on a larger scale. Four 23-ton iron anchor plates, one for each of the four cables, were positioned at the bottom of both anchorages. Eighteen 12-foot-long eyebars radiated from the center of each plate, forming the first link in a double-tiered eyebar chain extending to the top of the anchorage. As the successive links of the chain were attached to each other they were encased in masonry. At the top, the number of eyebars in the last link of the chain was increased to thirty-eight, and each of the nineteen strands of wire that made up each cable was pinned between a pair of eyebars.

Diagram of anchor chains
Appleton's Journal
Courtesy: Rensselaer Polytechnic Institute Archives, New York

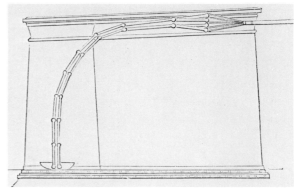

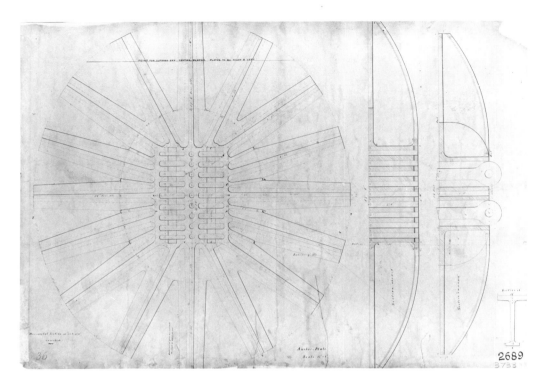

Left:
Francis Collingwood
American, 1834-1911
Plan and Elevation of Anchor Plate n.d.
Black ink and colored ink on paper
67.0 x 99.1 cm. (26⅜ x 39 in.)
Collection: Municipal Archives of the City of New York, inv. no. 3733

Below:
G. W. Pach
Brooklyn Anchorage
October 25, 1878
Collection: Museum of the City of New York

Right:
G. W. Pach
New York Anchorage near Completion n.d.
Collection: Museum of the City of New York

After the cables were firmly secured, the last masonry courses were added to the anchorages and the 60,000-ton anchorage structures were complete. Each anchorage measures 119 by 129 feet at its base and 104 by 117 feet at the roadway level.

Below:
G. W. Pach
Approach under Construction n.d.
Collection: Museum of the City of New York

VANDEWATER STR.

Made up of nine different bridges over the waterfront streets of New York and Brooklyn, the approaches provide access to the Bridge's main span. They are constructed of granite-faced brick on a limestone foundation and measure 971 feet to the Brooklyn anchorage and 1,562½ feet to the New York anchorage. By 1877, when work on the approaches began, $3.8 million had been spent buying up the land over which they would run.

Wilhelm Hildenbrand
Approach, Chatham Street to
Anchorage (detail) 1877
Black ink and colored ink on paper
Collection: Municipal Archives of the City of New York, inv. no. 4121G

47

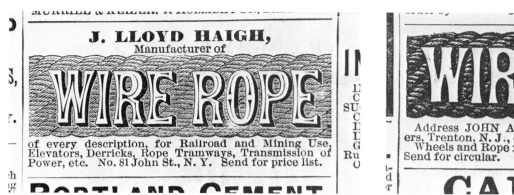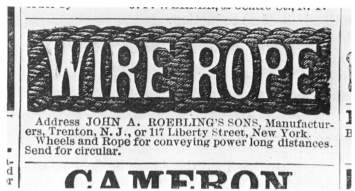

Wire rope advertisements for J. Lloyd Haigh and John A. Roebling's Sons
Scientific American, 1876
Courtesy: Columbia University, New York

The saga of the award of the contract for the Bridge's cable wire was a sad and disturbing one for Washington Roebling. In the fall of 1876 Roebling liquidated his holdings in the Roebling wireworks so that the company could compete in the bidding; that December John A. Roebling's Sons was given a contract to supply wire made of Bessemer steel. In January 1877, however, the Bridge board decided that crucible-cast steel was wanted instead, and J. Lloyd Haigh got the work with the lowest bid. Roebling doubted the strength and quality of Haigh's wire, and, sure enough, on Thanksgiving Day, 1877, a wire broke. It was discovered that Haigh had been substituting lengths of faulty wire for ones which had passed inspection, and using Bessemer steel while charging for the more expensive crucible-cast kind. Nonetheless, he continued to supply the wire for the Bridge's main cables. Roebling claimed this was because Abram Hewitt, a member of the Bridge board, was getting a ten percent kickback on Haigh's payment in exchange for not foreclosing on a mortgage he held on Haigh's wireworks. In designing the main cables, Roebling had called for wire six times stronger than necessary. He calculated that Haigh's faulty wire was still five times stronger than needed and that there was, therefore, no cause for alarm. Later, however, when it came time to wrap the main cables and hang the suspenders, John A. Roebling's Sons made the wire.

Telegram to Washington A. Roebling
August 14, 1876
Collection: Rensselaer Polytechnic Institute Archives, New York

Washington Roebling was recuperating from caisson disease at his home in Trenton, New Jersey, when his master mechanic E. Frank Farrington wired him on August 14, 1876, with the news that two "travelers" had been fished out of the East River. Spliced together at their ends, these two ropes formed

an "endless traveler" that served as a sort of giant conveyer belt between the anchorages. Worked back and forth through a system of pulleys by a steam engine, the traveler could transport men and wire across the river. On August 25, Farrington, who had worked with both Roeblings on the Niagara and Cincinnati bridges, had the honor of being the first man to cross the river using this rope. Riding in a boatswain's chair hanging from the traveler (see illustration on page 135), he waved gamely to an estimated 10,000 spectators as the rope pulled him along.

After a second endless traveler had been hung, several other ropes were strung across the river—some to support a footbridge, others to hold the 40-foot-long, 4-foot-wide platforms on which the men would stand when binding the wires of the main cables. With the travelers, the footbridge, and the platforms in place, cable spinning began, and the travelers demonstrated their main function.

The steel wire for the cables was wound on 8-foot-wide drums each containing ten miles of wire spliced together. These drums were placed on the Brooklyn anchorage. To send a length of wire to the other side, workmen first looped the wire around a "carrier wheel" hung from the traveler, and then attached the wire to a horseshoe-shaped "shoe" on the anchorage. The traveler then pulled the wheel carrying the wire to New York, where the wire was taken off the wheel and secured to another shoe. Because the traveler formed a loop, two lengths of wire could be strung at once. As one carrier wheel transported a wire to New York, another carrier wheel returned empty to Brooklyn to pick up more wire. Men on the platforms adjusted each wire after it was spun to insure that all the wires in the cable were parallel. The trip from anchorage to anchorage took about ten minutes.

When about 280 wires had been strung together, they were bound at fifteen-inch intervals and became a strand. When nineteen strands had been made, they were wrapped with wire to form a cable. Each cable contained 3,515 miles of wire.

Above:
Travelers, footbridge, and platforms in place for cable spinning
April 1877
Collection: Museum of the City of New York

Below:
Carrier wheel
Collection: Rensselaer Polytechnic Institute Archives, New York

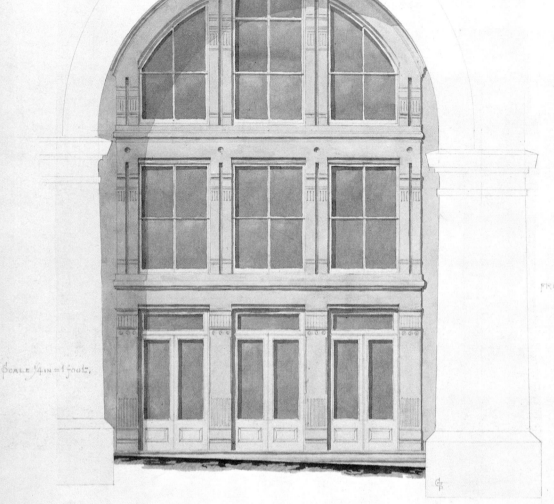

DESIGN FOR IRON FRONTS

FILLING ARCHES & SPACES BETWEEN PIERS

NEW YORK SIDE OF N.Y. & B.N BRIDGE.

FROM J.B. & J.M. CORNELL.

BUILDERS IN IRON.

NEW YORK.

SCALE ¼IN = 1 FOOT.

6198

3280

77

Anonymous
Iron Fronts of Warehouses,
Bridge Approach n.d.
Black ink on paper
57.8 × 47.63 cm.
(22¾ × 18¾ in.)
Collection: Municipal Archives of the
City of New York, inv. no. 6198

John A. Roebling and
Wilhelm Hildenbrand
**General Plan and Elevation of the
Bridge** 1867
Black ink and colored ink
on paper
78.1 × 420.37 cm.
(30¾ × 165½ in.)
*Collection: Municipal Archives of the
City of New York, inv. no. 149A*

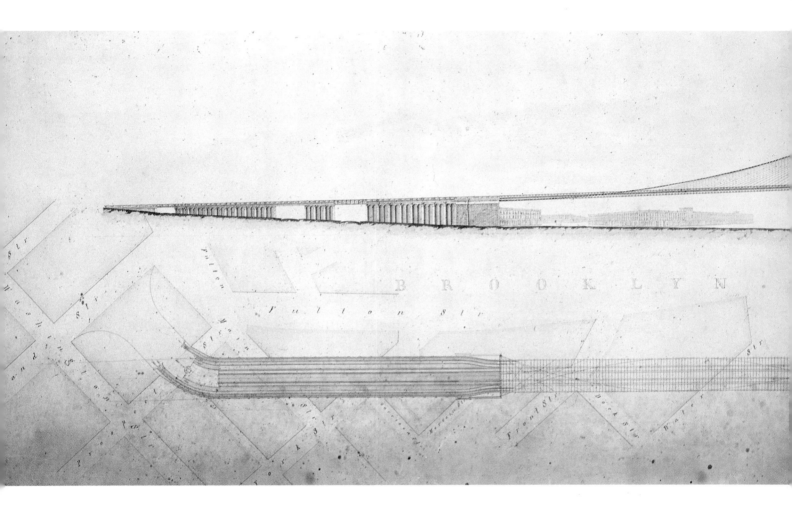

69 B

Wilhelm Hildenbrand
Bridge Approach, Chatham Street,
New York *(detail)* April 26, 1877
Black ink and colored ink
on paper
Collection: The Municipal Archives of
the City of New York, inv. no. 4121C

51

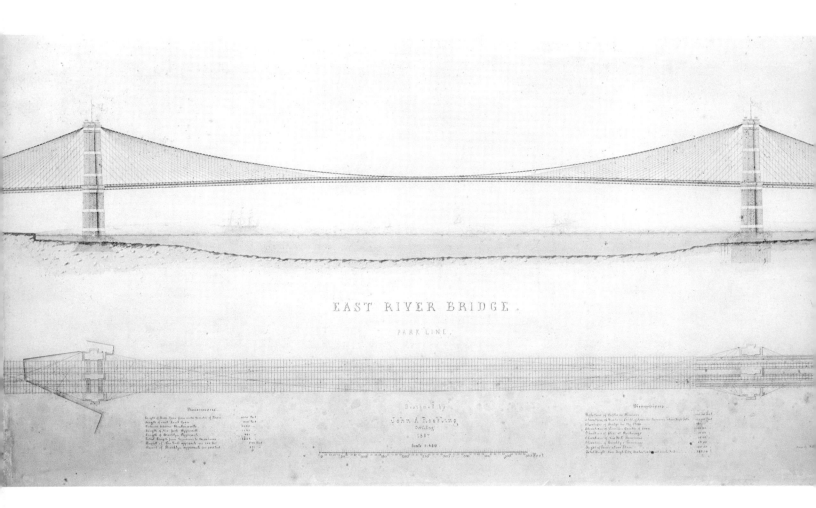

EAST RIVER BRIDGE.

PARK LINE.

BROOKLYN BRIDGE: CHRONOLOGY OF CONSTRUCTION

Center line surveys begun:	June 1869
Ground broken for Brooklyn tower foundation:	January 3, 1870
Brooklyn caisson launched:	March 19, 1870
Brooklyn caisson towed to position:	May 3 and 4, 1870
Work commenced inside Brooklyn caisson:	May 21, 1870
First stone laid on Brooklyn foundation:	June 15, 1870
Fire in Brooklyn caisson:	December 1, 1870
Brooklyn foundation completed:	March 11, 1871
New York caisson launched:	May 8, 1871
New York caisson towed to position:	September 11, 1871
Roebling stops descent of New York caisson:	May 18, 1872
New York tower foundation completed:	July 12, 1872
Brooklyn anchorage begun:	February 1873
New York anchorage begun:	May 1875
Brooklyn tower completed:	June 1875
Brooklyn anchorage completed:	November 1875
New York tower completed:	July 1876
New York anchorage completed:	July 1876
First wire for cable making stretched:	August 14, 1876
E. F. Farrington makes first crossing:	August 25, 1876
First cable wire run out:	May 29, 1877
Cable making begun:	June 11, 1877
Cable spinning completed:	October 5, 1878
Understructure for bridge floor completed:	December 1881
Trusswork and promenade completed:	April 1883
Bridge opened:	May 24, 1883

Launching weight, Brooklyn caisson:	3,000 tons
Launching weight, New York caisson:	3,250 tons
Height of Brooklyn caisson when launched:	14 feet 6 inches
Height of Brooklyn caisson when completed:	21 feet 6 inches
Height of New York caisson when launched:	14 feet 6 inches
Height of New York caisson when completed:	31 feet 6 inches
Size of each tower at high-water mark:	140 feet by 59 feet
Size of each tower at top:	136 feet by 53 feet
Total height of each tower above high water:	276 feet 6 inches
Height of roadway at towers:	119 feet
Height of arches above roadway:	117 feet
Height of towers above roadway:	159 feet
Width of openings through towers:	33 feet 9 inches
Total masonry in Brooklyn tower:	38,214 cubic yards
Total masonry in New York tower:	46,945 cubic yards
Size of each anchorage at base:	129 feet by 119 feet
Size of each anchorage at top:	117 feet by 104 feet
Height of anchorages in front:	89 feet
Height of anchorages in rear:	85 feet
Weight of each anchorage:	60,000 tons
Total number of anchor plates:	8
Weight of each anchor plate:	23 tons
Weight of suspended superstructure from anchorage to anchorage, 3,400 feet:	6,620 tons
Total weight of the bridge (exclusive of masonry):	14,680 tons
Grade of roadway:	3¼ feet in 100 feet

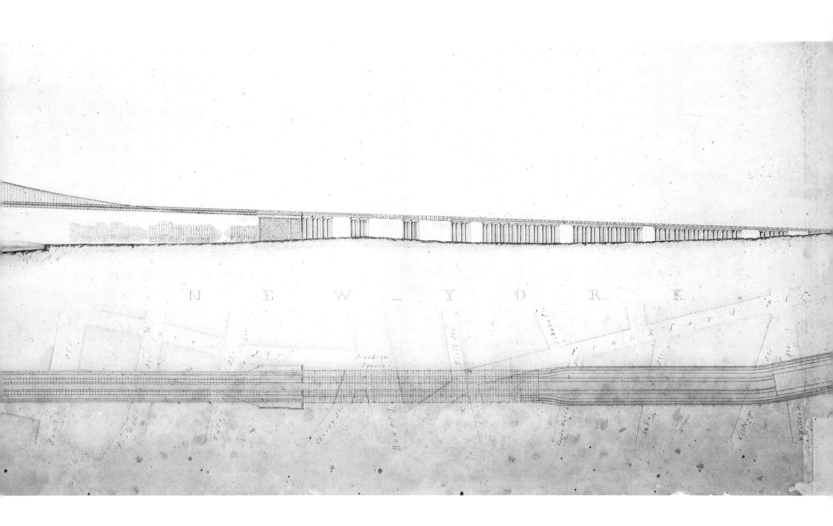

VITAL STATISTICS 1883

Length of river span:	1,595 feet 6 inches
Length of each land span:	930 feet
Length of Brooklyn approach:	971 feet
Length of New York approach:	1,562 feet 6 inches
Total length of Bridge:	5,989 feet
Full width of Bridge floor:	85 feet
Number of cables:	4
Diameter of each cable:	15¾ inches
Length of each cable:	3,578 feet 6 inches
Number of wires in each cable:	5,434
Total length of wire in each cable:	3,515 miles
Miles of wrapping wire on each cable:	243 miles 943 feet
Weight of each cable:	1,732,086 pounds
Ultimate strength of each cable:	24,621,780 pounds
Number of suspenders from each cable, main span:	208
Number of suspenders from each cable, each land span:	86
Strength of each suspender:	70 tons
Greatest weight on a single suspender:	10 tons
Greatest weight on a single cable:	3,000 tons
Depth of Brooklyn foundation below high water:	44 feet 6 inches
Depth of New York foundation below high water:	78 feet 6 inches
Size of Brooklyn caisson:	168 feet by 102 feet
Size of New York caisson:	172 feet by 102 feet

Above:
Trade card *circa* 1875
Chromolithograph
8.3 x 17.5 cm. (3¼ x 6⅞ in.)
*Collection: The New-York Historical
Society*

The prospect of cable spinning,
and the matrix of steel wire that
would result, clearly excited the
brilliant graphic artist who
designed this card the year before
the actual spinning began.

Below:
Silas A. Holmes
**Engineers and Superintendent on the 5th Course of
Tower Masonry above Roadway, Brooklyn Pier**
November 1872
Collection: Museum of the City of New York

A team of skilled and dedicated engineers and
administrators ensured that Washington Roebling's
directions would be correctly executed. The numbered
figures pictured here are: 1, E. Frank Farrington, master
mechanic; 2, William C. Kingsley, general superintendent;
3, Orestes P. Quintard, bookkeeper; 4, Alex McKinnon,
foreman of masons on the Brooklyn tower; 5, Francis
Collingwood, assistant engineer; 6, George W. McNulty,
assistant engineer; 7, Thomas G. Douglas, head mason;
and 8, William H. Paine, assistant engineer.

View of Bridge towers from the New York side *circa* 1876-77
Stereograph
Collection: The New-York Historical Society

Workmen crossing the footbridge from Brooklyn to New York 1877

Francis H. Schell
American, 1834-1909
and **Thomas Hogan**
American
Promenade in Mid-air: The Brooklyn Ascent to the Bridge Tower
Harper's Weekly, March 31, 1877

55

J. R. LeRoy
View of Cable Spinning n.d.
*Collection: Museum of the City of
New York*

Below:
Cable spinning n.d.
*Collection: Museum of the City of
New York*

Snapping cables 1878
New York Illustrated Times

Cable spinning was progressing
smoothly until one day in June of
1878 when a strand snapped,
swinging snake-like across the
river. Two men were killed and
several were injured.

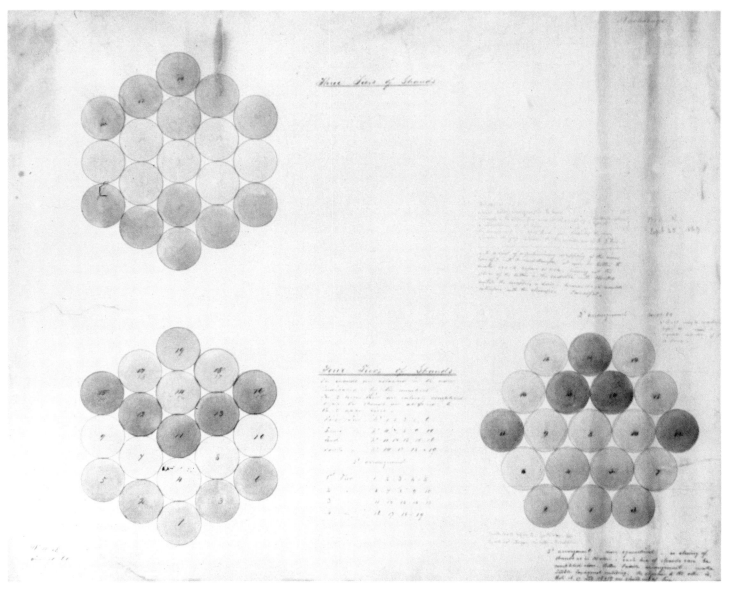

Above:
Washington A. Roebling
and **George McNulty**
American, *circa* 1845-1924
Variations on Strand Arrangements for the Cable 1869
Includes notes of 1872 and 1875
Black ink and watercolor on paper
56.5 x 78.7 cm. (22¼ x 31 in.)
Collection: Rensselaer Polytechnic Institute Archives, New York

Washington Roebling and George McNulty studied
various configurations for arranging the nineteen strands
which made up each cable. The arrangement that was
used is closest to the diagram on the lower right.

Below:
Charles Pollack
**View of Cables from the New
York Tower** n.d.
*Collection: Museum of the City of
New York*

Each cable rests in 4-foot-high, u-shaped saddles below the roofs of the towers. The saddles are placed on rollers, providing the cables some flexibility to adapt to changes in load. The diagonal stays are attached to the towers at a point just below the saddles.

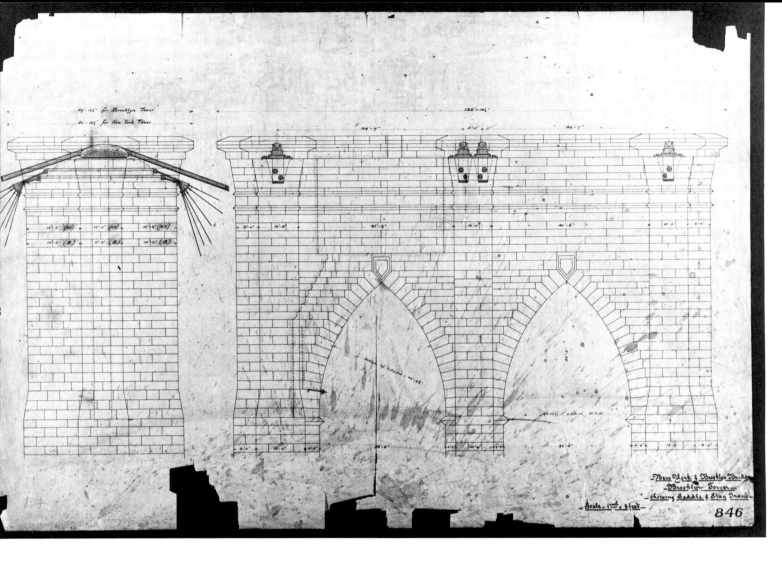

Above:
Washington A. Roebling
and **Wilhelm Hildenbrand**
Brooklyn Tower, Saddles and Stay Irons
April 23, 1873
Black ink, colored ink, and pencil
on linen
100.6 x 55.6 cm. (39⅝ x 21⅞ in.)
*Collection: Municipal Archives of the City of
New York, inv. no. 7813*

Below:
Entries to the saddles and stay irons n.d.
*Collection: Rensselaer Polytechnic Institute
Archives, New York*

Right:
The cable saddles n.d.
(two views)
Collection: The Brooklyn Museum, New York

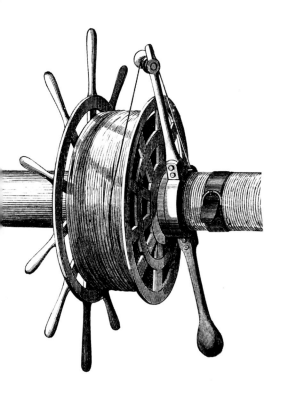

After the nineteen strands of a cable had been lashed together in their proper relation to one another, the cable was wrapped with soft wire and coated with white lead. The wrapping device, developed by John Roebling, was placed on a buggy that could accommodate the four men needed to perform the operation.

Above and right:
Cable-wrapping machine and cable wrapping
Scientific American
November 9, 1878
Courtesy: Columbia University, New York

Cable wrapping
Harper's New Monthly Magazine, May 1883

**Attachment of steel-rope
suspenders from cables** n.d.
Harper's Weekly

Men moving with monkey-like
agility attached five-inch-wide iron
bands with sockets to the cables;
from these were hung the
suspenders. As E. Frank
Farrington told a reporter after his
historic trip across the river on the
traveler rope, "no man can be a
bridge builder who must educate
his nerves."

Suspending the floor beams
Scientific American
May 21, 1881
*Collection: Rensselaer Polytechnic
Institute Archives, New York*

Right:
Construction of Bridge floor, looking towards New York 1881
Collection: Museum of the City of New York

Below:
Bridge floor under construction with six unidentified men on the footbridge n.d.
Collection: The New-York Historical Society

Composed entirely of steel, the Bridge floor represented a major industrial and technological innovation. No structure of such size had ever been built of steel, and the contractor had to design new machinery in order to manufacture the girders.

The floor was formed from open-work girders, or trusses, which are lighter and stronger than solid beams. The principal trusses were hung from the suspender cables, parallel to the towers, 7 feet 6 inches apart, with smaller trusses suspended halfway between. Bolted to these trusses at right angles were six rows of other trusses running the length of the Bridge. The floor was constructed from the towers and the anchorages outwards; as each girder was secured to the suspenders, planks were laid on top, creating a working platform for the suspension of the next section of floor.

Right:
Bridge floor construction
Die Gartenlaube, 1881
Collection: Rensselaer Polytechnic Institute Archives, New York

George Brainard
American, *circa* 1845-1887
New York and Brooklyn Bridge
circa 1882
*Collection: Brooklyn Public Library,
New York*

The diagonal stays, which cross the vertical suspenders to create a web of wire, have, like the towers, inspired countless artists and writers. The hypoteneuse of a right triangle formed by each stay in combination with the tower and roadway symbolized for Roebling the same sort of metaphysical harmony with nature as did the catenary curve of the main cables. At the same time the stays were essential to the overall strength of the Bridge.

Hundreds of stays span out from each tower to relieve the suspenders of some of the load. They are secured fifteen feet apart to the Bridge floor and are clamped to the suspenders to further stiffen the structure. It has been calculated that the diagonal stays alone could support the roadway.

Below:
William Vanderbosch
and **Wilhelm Hildenbrand**
**Diagonal Stays and
Superstructure with Calculations
for Brooklyn Side** n.d.
Black ink, red ink, and pencil
on paper
63.8 × 94.0 cm. (25⅛ × 37 in.)
*Collection: Municipal Archives of the
City of New York, inv. no. 7157*

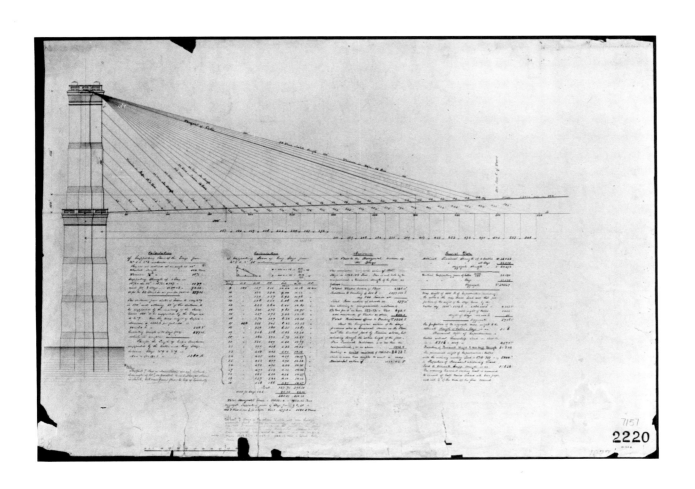

2220

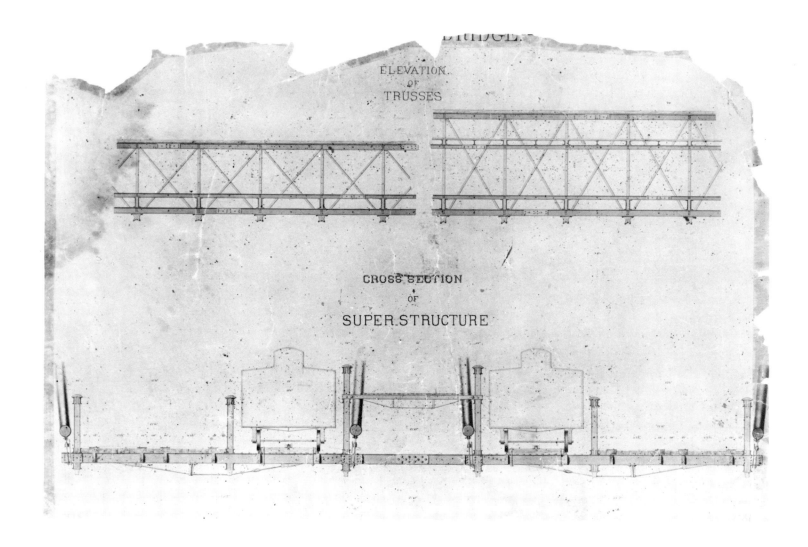

ELEVATION
OF
TRUSSES

CROSS SECTION
OF
SUPER STRUCTURE

Above:
Washington A. Roebling
and **William Vanderbosch**
Superstructure Elevation and
Cross Section Showing Trusses
with Location of Train Tracks and
Promenade
April 25, 1870
Black ink, colored ink, and
watercolor on paper
58.4 × 84.8 cm. (23 × 33⅜ in.),
irregular
Collection: Municipal Archives of the
City of New York, inv. no. 7381

Right:
Breading G. Way
American, d. 1940
Brooklyn Bridge: View of
Promenade and Train Tracks *circa*
1888
Collection: Brooklyn Public Library,
New York

The Bridge's pedestrian promenade was built eighteen feet above the roadway. John Roebling thought of it as an important urban amenity. "I need not state," he wrote in his original plan, "that in a crowded commercial city, such a promenade will be of incalcuable value." The walkway was intended and has always been used as a place to exercise, socialize, relax on a bench, and enjoy the view of the city and river. It is more like a park than a street.

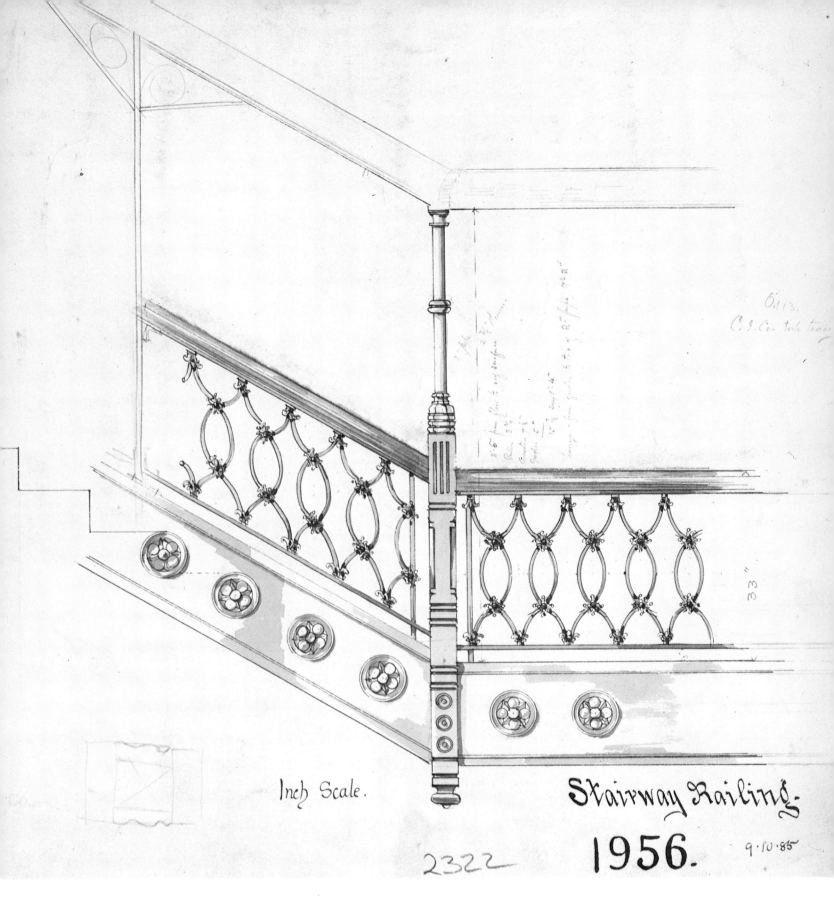

Inch Scale.

Stairway Railing.

1956.

9·10·85

2322

Anonymous
Stairway Railing
September 10, 1885
Black ink, watercolor, and pencil
on paper
39.4 × 33.0 cm. (15½ × 13 in.)
Collection: Municipal Archives of the
City of New York, inv. no. 2322

65

Facing page:
Wrench
66.0 × 30.5 × 2.5 cm.
(26 × 12 × 1 in.)
Collection: New York City
Bureau of Highway Operations

When the Bridge was built there
were no standard-size wrenches
available that were large enough
for the bolts. Specially constructed
tools like this one had to be made.

"The promenade," E. Frank Farrington wrote, "is over fifteen feet wide, and
so high that pedestrians will have an uninterrupted view of their
surroundings. Invalids will here find the purest air and the brightest
sunshine—when it shines anywhere at all. Here the orator and the poet will
come for inspiration. Here Chawles and Arabella Seraphina will plight their
faith, while Hezekiah and Jerusha from the back country will make this the
terminus of their wedding 'tower'."

Anonymous
Bridge Promenade *circa* 1883
29.2 × 21.6 cm. (11½ × 8½ in.)
Collection: Municipal Archives of the
City of New York

Anonymous
Construction of Bridge
Promenade
late 1882 or early 1883
29.2 × 21.0 cm. (11½ × 8¼ in.)
Collection: Municipal Archives of the
City of New York

69

Left:
Daniel Berry Austin
Bridge Promenade
circa 1883
Collection: Brooklyn Public
Library, New York

Right:
Anonymous
Bird's-Eye View of Bridge
May 25, 1883
Collection: Municipal Archives
of the City of New York

Below:
George P. Hall and Sons
Vista of Bridge from
Brooklyn Side n.d.
16.5 × 68.3 cm.
(6½ × ⅞ in.)
Collection: Municipal Archives
of the City of New York

Facing page, top:
Anonymous
Bird's-Eye View of the
Great Suspension Bridge
1883
Color lithograph
38.7 × 62.2 cm.
(15¼ × 24¼ in.)
Published by The Judge
Publishing Company
Collection: Leonard Milberg,
New York

BIRD'S-EYE VIEW OF THE GREAT SUSPENSION BRIDGE.

CONNECTING THE CITIES OF NEW YORK AND BROOKLYN, FROM NEW YORK LOOKING SOUTH-EAST.

John Mackie Falconer
American, 1820-1903
Fireworks at the Opening of the Brooklyn Bridge 1883
Oil on canvas board
17.8 x 25.1 cm. (7 x 9⅞ in.)
Collection: The Long Island Historical Society, New York

The Bridge's opening day, proclaimed People's Day, produced a frenzy of festivity unlike anything seen before. People poured into New York and Brooklyn by train, boat, and barge, and all the hotels were full. At noon, business virtually shut down, and President Chester A. Arthur and New York Governor Grover Cleveland led a parade down Broadway for the official opening. At 2 p.m., the President and his party began their walk across the Bridge as a band played "Hail to the Chief," the North Atlantic Squadron fired a salute, and church bells tolled. Emily Roebling, representing her invalid husband, waited for the President at the Brooklyn terminal with Brooklyn Mayor Seth Low and several thousand invited guests. Later the President and the Governor went to personally congratulate Washington Roebling at his Brooklyn Heights home.

At eight p.m., with the Bridge cleared of all traffic, fifty great rockets began the climactic pyrotechnic display—an event recorded by the artist John Mackie Falconer as it appeared from the foot of Remsen Street in Brooklyn. While bells and whistles and cheers sounded from every direction, fireworks were dropped from gas balloons, shot off the Bridge, fired from boats, and set off over land. For the grand finale, five hundred rockets were fired simultaneously. All told, fourteen tons were exploded.

Anonymous
Fireworks off the Bridge 1883
Watercolor, pastel, and pencil
on paper
59.1 x 47.3 cm. (23¼ x 18⅝ in.)
Collection: Municipal Archives of the
City of New York, inv. no. 150A
Photo Courtesy: American Heritage

Drawn for the Unexcelled
Fireworks Company.

73

"Could there be a more astounding exhibition of the power of man to change the face of nature," New York Congressman Abram Hewitt asked in his opening-day speech, "than the panoramic view which presents itself to the spectator standing upon the crowning arch of the Bridge . . . In no previous period of the world's history could this Bridge have been built. Within the last hundred years the greater part of the knowledge necessary for its erection has been gained . . . At the ocean gateway of such a nation, well may stand the stately figure of Liberty enlightening the world; and in hope and faith, as well as gratitude, we write upon the towers of our beautiful Bridge, to be illuminated by her electric ray, the words of exultation, Finis Coronat Opus."

Top:
Finis Coronat Opus 1883
(The End Crowns the Work)
Collection: The Brooklyn Museum, New York

Above:
Currier and Ives
The Great East River
Suspension Bridge *circa* 1883
Color lithograph
87.6 x 53.4 cm. (34½ x 21 in.)
Collection: The Long Island Historical Society, New York

74

Left:
Invitation to the opening of the New York and Brooklyn Bridge
1883
16.5 x 22.9 cm. (6½ x 9 in.)
Private Collection, New York

Above:
Anonymous
Bird's-eye View of the Great New York and Brooklyn Bridge and
Grand Display of Fireworks on Opening Night 1883
Color lithograph published by A. Major
38.7 x 62.2 cm. (15¼ x 24½ in.)
Collection: Leonard Milberg, New York

Below:
Frederick Burr Opper
American, 1857-?
The Grand Opening March over
the Brooklyn Bridge
Puck, May 23, 1883
Color lithograph
32.4 x 48.9 cm. (12¾ x 19¼ in.)
*Collection: The Long Island Historical
Society, New York*

On Decoration Day, 1883, a week after the Bridge opened, huge holiday crowds turned out to enjoy the promenade in perfect spring weather. About 20,000 people were on the Bridge in the early afternoon when a crush of traffic from both directions effectively stopped all movement on the narrow stairs on the New York side. Someone tripped, there were screams, and a panic ensued in which twelve people were trampled to death.

The Brooklyn Bridge horror
Illustrated Police News, May 30, 1883

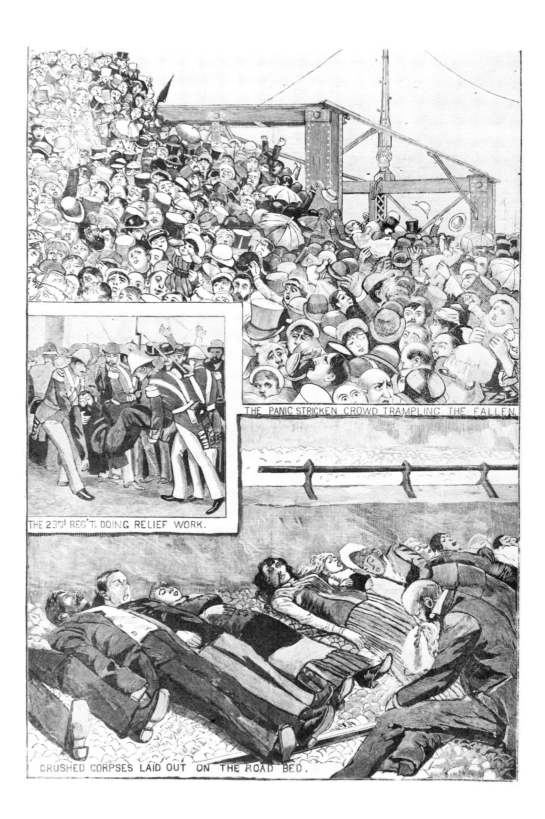

THE PANIC STRICKEN CROWD TRAMPLING THE FALLEN.

THE 23ʳᵈ REG'T. DOING RELIEF WORK.

CRUSHED CORPSES LAID OUT ON THE ROAD BED.

Bridge crush
Harper's Weekly, May 31, 1883

The first leap from Brooklyn Bridge
Brooklyn *Daily Eagle*, 1885

On May 19, 1885, Robert E. Odlum became the first man to seek immortality by leaping from the Bridge. Although he was an experienced athlete and a swimming instructor, he was killed by the impact of the 135-foot fall.

Steve Brodie's leap to fame
Brooklyn *Daily Eagle*, 1886

On July 23, 1886, Steve Brodie claimed he had jumped from the Bridge and survived. He was pulled from the water, but no one actually saw him jump and it is most likely he never did. Still, the purported leap made him a celebrity and the subject of a hit play called *On the Bowery*. The first documented survivor of a jump was Larry Donovan.

Steve Brodie n.d.
Collection: The Brooklyn Museum, New York

Above:
Charles Bierstadt
American, *circa* 1819-1903
New York Harbor from the Statue of Liberty *circa* 1890
Artotype
Collection: The New-York Historical Society

Right:
John Mackie Falconer
American, 1820-1903
From the Shore of Brooklyn, Long Island 1882
Etching
23.5 x 34.0 cm. (9¼ x 13¼ in.)
Collection: New York Etching Club, William Frost Mobley Collection

William Bliss Baker
American, 1859-1886
**View of New York Harbor with
Brooklyn Bridge in the Distance**
1883
Oil on canvas
91.4 x 127.0 cm. (36 x 50 in.)
Private Collection, Michigan

Even before the Bridge was opened, New York stores and industries used it
in advertisements associating their products or services with the Bridge's
strength and fame. Soon after it was completed, images of the Bridge began
appearing on furnishings ranging from lamps to wallpaper.

Above:
Charles Parsons
American, 1821-1910
and **Lyman W. Atwater**
American, 1835-1891
Mulford, Cary and Conklin
Leather and Findings Poster 1877
Chromolithograph
(Currier and Ives)
61.6 x 83.5 cm. (24¼ x 32⅞ in.)
Collection: The New-York Historical
Society

Facing page, top:
Colored, engraved trade card
circa 1880
10.8 x 16.5 cm. (4¼ x 6½ in.)
Collection: The New-York Historical
Society

Facing page, bottom:
Engraved trade card 1888
7.9 x 13.0 cm. (3⅛ x 5⅛ in.)
Collection: The New-York Historical
Society

The Great Suspension Bridge between New York and Brooklyn, New York Elevated Rail Road etc.

LENGTH OF RIVER SPAN 1.595-6 IN, TOTAL LENGTH OF BRIDGE 5 989 Ft. WIDTH OF BRIDGE 85 Ft.

HEIGHT OF BRIDGE IN CENTER OF RIVER SPAN 135 Ft. HEIGHT OF TOWERS ABOVE HIGH WATER 278 Ft. DEPTH OF TOWER FOUNDATION BELOW HIGH WATER, NEW YORK 78 Ft. BROOKLYN 45 Ft.

COST OF BRIDGE ABOUT $15,000,000.

CONSTRUCTION COMMENCED, JANUARY 1870, FINISHED 1883.

FAHYS COIN No 1

NEW YORK AND BROOKLYN BRIDGE.

Entered according to Act of Congress in the year 1868 by Joseph Fahys & Co. in the Office of the Librarian of Congress at Washington

83

Above, and facing page:
Chromolithograph fan 1883
Made for the Cowperthwait
Furniture Company
Diameter: 22.9 cm. (9 in.)
*Collection: The New-York Historical
Society*

**Tumbler with scenes of the
Brooklyn Bridge, The Brooklyn
Museum, and Grand Army Plaza**
circa 1900
Porcelain
Height: 9.5 cm. (3¾ in.)
*Collection: The Brooklyn Museum,
New York*

Ernest Ankener and
George McNulty
American, 1845-1924
**Gable-End Elevation, Brooklyn
Bridge Station, Brooklyn
Terminal** October 13, 1882
Black ink, colored ink, and pencil
on paper
67.9 x 98.1 cm. (26¾ x 38⅝ in.)
*Collection: Municipal Archives of the
City of New York, inv. no. 1152*

The rapid growth of the city of Brooklyn in the mid-nineteenth century made clear the urgent need for a dependable transit link with New York. From 1810 to the end of the Civil War in 1865, Brooklyn's population increased from 3,000 to almost 300,000. In 1870, the year construction of the Bridge began, fourteen ferries transported 37,000 passengers a day between the two cities. By 1883, 112,000 passengers were being carried.

Washington Roebling had initially opposed a heavy railway for the Bridge because he felt the concentrated load of a large locomotive would impose too much additional stress on the structure. He preferred instead a cable railway of tried and proven design similar to the system his father had used to move barges across the Pennsylvania canal portages. The cable cars were drawn by an endless steel wire rope driven by steam engines. There were terminals at both ends of the Bridge where passengers paid their five-cent fare and climbed a staircase to the train platform. When service

Left:
Anonymous
Brooklyn Station, Prospect Street,
under Construction circa 1881
31.8 x 42.9 cm. (12½ x 16⅞ in.)
Collection: Municipal Archives of the
City of New York, inv. no. 383

Below:
Anonymous
Station Roof circa 1886
19.1 x 24.1 cm. (7½ x 9½ in.)
Collection: Municipal Archives of the
City of New York, inv. no. 87

commenced on September 24, 1883, there were twenty-four cars in operation and the trip across took five minutes. Six million passengers were carried that first year. By 1888 the number was 31 million, and the service was severely overburdened. With Roebling's consent, eight steam locomotives were put into service.

In 1898, the year Brooklyn was incorporated into New York City, tracks for electric trolleys were laid on the Bridge and electric trains of the Brooklyn Elevated Company began running on the cable car tracks (replacing the cable cars except during rush hours). Ten years later, with half a million passengers crossing the Bridge each day, the cable cars were totally eliminated and their tracks were reinforced to permit expanded service of the electric trains. The trains continued running until 1944, the trolleys until 1950.

New York entrance
Harper's Weekly, May 26, 1883
Private Collection, New York

Francis H. Schell
American, 1834-1909
and **Thomas Hogan**
American
**The New York and Brooklyn
Suspension Bridge, Brooklyn
Entrance**
Harper's Weekly, May 26, 1983
*Courtesy: Museum of the City of
New York*

Below:
**Anonymous
New York and Brooklyn Bridge,
New York Terminal** 1889
12.7 x 17.8 cm. (5 x 7 in.)
Private Collection, New York

Above:
George Brainard
American, 1845-1887
Bridge Railroad Tracks *circa* 1886
20.3 x 25.4 cm. (8 x 10 in.)
Collection: Brooklyn Public Library,
New York

Right:
New York and Brooklyn Bridge
Railroad ticket n.d.
2.5 x 3.8 cm. (1 x 1½ in.) irregular
Collection: Museum of the City of
New York

90

Top:
Promenade, railway, and roadway
Scientific American n.d.
Courtesy: Columbia University,
New York

Above:
Anonymous
View of Manhattan from
Brooklyn Tower *circa* 1883
14.3 x 40.3 cm. (5⅝ x 15⅞ in.)
Collection: Municipal Archives of the
City of New York

Left:
Cable engines 1884
Colection: Museum of the City of
New York   91

George Brainard
American, 1845-1887
New York and Brooklyn Bridge
circa 1888
20.3 x 25.4 cm. (8 x 10 in.)
Collection: Brooklyn Public Library,
New York

Right:
Breading G. Way
American, d. 1940
New York and Brooklyn Bridge
circa 1888
20.3 x 25.4 cm. (8 x 10 in.)
Collection: Brooklyn Public Library,
New York

Below:
Stock certificate 1880
Collection: The Long Island Historical
Society, New York

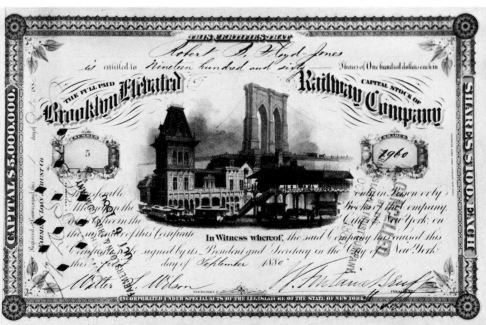

92

Left:
Anonymous
New York and Brooklyn Bridge,
Train at Sand Street *circa* 1890
Collection: The Brooklyn Museum,
New York

Below:
George P. Hall & Son
New York and Brooklyn Bridge,
Brooklyn Terminal 1898
19.1 x 24.8 cm. (7½ x 9¾ in.)
Collection: Municipal Archives of the
City of New York

Above:
Terminal at Park Row, New York, looking north n.d.
Collection: The New-York Historical Society

Right:
Bridge from the New York side
The New Metropolis, 1899
Courtesy: Museum of the City of New York

94

Above:
Brooklyn Bridge and Manhattan Bridge n.d.
Collection: Museum of the City of New York

In 1896 a British visitor struck by the density of advertising adorning the walls of buildings near the Bridge noted that many of the ads seemed to be for one particular product. "Its spirited proprietors have bought up every wall in New York that faces towards the Brooklyn Bridge," the visitor wrote. "As you stand there the red houses seem to be laced with gold letters; the whole city is yelling aloud concerning the virtues of Castoria."

Left:
Brooklyn *Daily Eagle* Bridge Crush March
January 29, 1907
Sheet music
Private Collection, New York

Proposed train loop for the Brooklyn Bridge
Scientific American, March 18, 1905
Private Collection, New York

In 1905, *Scientific American* published a futuristic scheme to facilitate the flow of passengers using the Bridge trains. This scheme, proposed by an engineer named Edward Curtiss, envisioned circular rotating platforms 400 feet in diameter for each terminal. An endless train of light cars, which would be moved across the Bridge at ten miles per hour by an electric cable system, would engage with these platforms and turn them. Passengers would reach the rotating platforms by staircases, entering at the center where the motion would be slight. At the edge of the platform where passengers entered or exited the train, there would be no difference in relative motion between train and platform. This imaginative design would have allowed a doubling of passenger capacity on the Bridge if the speed were kept at ten miles per hour, and twice that if the speed were increased to twenty miles per hour. "All the time now wasted by stopping, starting, backing, switching and waiting trains," Curtiss argued, "would be devoted to moving the people over the Bridge."

Illustration to Dr. Hillis's talk
Brooklyn *Daily Eagle*,
April 12, 1912
Courtesy: Rensselaer Polytechnic Institute Archives, New York

The City Beautiful movement, which was a major force in urban design in the decades before and after the turn of the century, was concerned with the planning of mass transportation, the building of grand public spaces, and the construction of monumental architecture inspired by Classical and Renaissance forms. These concerns were reflected in proposals involving the Bridge offered by a Brooklyn pastor named Dr. Newell Dwight Hillis and a New York City Bridge Commissioner named Arthur O'Keefe in 1912.

In a talk entitled "What Can We Do to Make Brooklyn a More Attractive City?" Dr. Hillis proposed building a shore highway and constructing an elevated promenade that would run from Joralemon Street to the Navy Yard while passing the entrances to the Brooklyn and Manhattan Bridges. This scheme foretold the construction of the Brooklyn-Queens Expressway and the Brooklyn Heights promenade.

Facing page, bottom:
Plan for the Redevelopment of Downtown Brooklyn *circa* 1912
Drawing by H. M. Pettit
India ink and wash touched with opaque white on paper
70.5 × 117.2 cm.
(27¾ × 46⅛ in.), sight
Collection: The Brooklyn Museum, New York, Gift of the Department of Public Works, Bureau of Bridges, City of New York

The proposal put forward by Commissioner O'Keefe was intended to improve the Brooklyn Bridge terminals, connect the Brooklyn Bridge to the Manhattan Bridge by a broad boulevard, and change the physical form of downtown Brooklyn. The streets from the Brooklyn Bridge to Brooklyn's Borough Hall would be cleared for a wide boulevard which would lead to a new civic center, and the elevated trains would be removed from the lower part of Brooklyn's Fulton Street. The Manhattan terminal would become a multileveled structure connecting to the city's underground subways.

Above:
Plan for the Redevelopment of Manhattan Terminal of the New York and Brooklyn Bridge
circa 1912
Drawing by H. M. Pettit
Indian ink and wash touched with opaque white on paper
67.9 × 140.3 cm.
(26¾ × 55¼ in.), sight
Collection: The Brooklyn Museum, New York, Gift of the Department of Public Works, Bureau of Bridges, City of New York

Silas A. Holmes
View of Brooklyn on Centerline
from the Top of the Brooklyn Pier
October 1872
Collection: Museum of the City of
New York

The origins of twentieth-century New York, both in its physical characteristics and its social institutions, can be traced to the years between 1870 and 1900. No single New York structure better symbolizes this era of progress and change than the Brooklyn Bridge. It embodies both the technological advances that were essential to the modernization of New York and the spirit of confidence that allowed designers, politicians, and the public to envision huge projects involving complicated administration and finance.

The New York of 1870 was a densely populated horizontal city in which the highest buildings were five and six stories. The great majority of people and commercial establishments were located below 23rd Street. Grand Central Depot, built between 1869 and 1871 (see page 102), was constructed at 42nd Street and Park Avenue in part because the city government had ruled that there could be no steam engines below that point—in other words, within the heart of the city.

By the 1880s some of the first skyscrapers had been built in lower Manhattan. Among the most notable was the Tribune building of 1873-75 (visible in the photograph at the top of the facing page). It combined advances in steel and iron construction with the passenger elevator to create the beginnings of the vertical city. In 1899 a British journalist wrote, "when they find themselves a little crowded, they simply tilt a street on end and call it a skyscraper."

The dazzle of New York at night was already a distinctive feature of the city when another British author told in 1882 of the electric lights on Broadway from 14th to 26th Street. "The effect of light in the squares of the

Above:
Anonymous
View of Manhattan from Brooklyn Tower, Bridge to the Right *circa* 1881
40.6 x 14.0 cm. (16 x 5½ in.)
Collection: Municipal Archives of the City of New York

Left:
George Schultz
Fulton Ferry and South Street n.d.
Collection: The New-York Historical Society

Currier and Ives
Liberty
Enlightening
the World 1886
Chromolithograph
78.7 x 52.1 cm.
(31 x 20½ in.)
Collection:
The New-York
Historical Society

THE GREAT BARTHOLDI STATUE.
LIBERTY ENLIGHTENING THE WORLD.
THE GIFT OF FRANCE TO THE AMERICAN PEOPLE.
ERECTED ON BEDLOE'S ISLAND NEW YORK HARBOR UNVEILED OCT. 28TH 1886

This magnificent colossal Statue (the largest ever known in the World) is of copper bronzed 151 feet in height and is mounted on a
Stone Pedestal 154 feet high, making the extreme height from foundation of Pedestal to the torch 305 feet. the height of the Statue from the
heel to the top of the head is 111 ft 6 in. Length of the hand 16 feet. Head from chin to cranium 17 ft 3 in. Breadth from ear to ear 10 feet, Length of
nose 4 ft 6 in. Length of right arm 42 feet. Circumference of arm 12 feet, Width of mouth 3 feet. Weight of Statue 450,000 pounds (225 tons) 40 persons can stand comfortably in the head and the torch will hold 12 people. The torch at night displays a powerful electric light and the great
Statue thus presents by night as by day an exceedingly grand and imposing appearance.

Empire City," this correspondent wrote, "can scarcely be described, so weird and so beautiful is it." The next year the electric lights on the Bridge were turned on, making it the first bridge in the world to be electrified.

The population density of lower Manhattan (330,000 persons per square mile on the Lower East Side by the late 1880s) was lessened somewhat by the development of apartment houses. The first of these houses, built for the middle class, were located north of the densest areas of the island. The famous Dakota apartment house, occupied in 1884, was so named, legend has it, because it was so far north and west of the central city that living there was like being in the Dakotas.

The effects of the crowded urban environment on people were addressed by such social reformers as Frederick Law Olmsted, who effected monumental change through his plans for New York's Central Park (designed in 1857), Brooklyn's Prospect Park (designed in 1866), and upper Manhattan's Riverside Park (designed and built between 1873 and 1910). These open spaces, planned in a naturalistic and picturesque style derived from nineteenth-century English landscape theory, gave the city dweller sorely needed room for mental and physical release. Olmsted theorized that parks were integral to a democracy: they served as places where all classes could mix and experience one another's company in an atmosphere lacking in the established social hierarchies. (For a comparison of the Bridge and Prospect Park see Albert Fein's essay.)

The development of these parks as important cultural institutions was paralleled by the establishment in the late 1800s of museums and libraries. The American Museum of Natural History was established in 1869, The Metropolitan Museum of Art was founded in 1870, and The Brooklyn Museum opened its doors in 1897. In 1895 the New York Public Library was founded, and two years later the Brooklyn Public Library Association began to serve the public. Both libraries were formed from the consolidation of private and semi-private libraries.

Above:
Dakota Apartments,
New York City *circa* 1895
Architect: Henry Hardenburgh
Completed 1884
Collection: Museum of the City of New York

Below:
Postcard of Central Park n.d.
Collection: Deborah Nevins, New York

Skating on the site of
Central Park 1859
Collection: Museum of the City of New York

Prospect Park,
the Vale of Cashmere n.d.
Courtesy: Olmsted Associates, Inc., Massachusetts

Grand Central Depot n.d.
Architect: John B. Snook
Completed 1871
Collection: Museum of the City of New York

The years after the Bridge opened brought radical physical and social change to Brooklyn. Although Brooklyn was known as New York's bedroom as early as the mid-1850s, the surge of immigration to New York in the 1880s pushed more and more people across the river. The neighborhoods of Park Slope and Prospect Heights were built up in the 1880s, and by the turn of the century development had moved further inland. Brooklyn was no longer just for Brooklynites: by the 1880s Coney Island was enjoyed by New Yorkers seeking release from the summer heat.

Essential to the development of both Brooklyn and New York was a sophisticated rapid transit system. By the end of the 1880s elevated railway lines had been established in both cities. Brooklyn also had electric trolleys (the dodging of which led to its baseball team's name) by the late 1880s, and Manhattan acquired them at the turn of the century. Manhattan's first subway, running from the Brooklyn Bridge to Grand Central to Times Square to 145th Street, opened in 1904. Construction of an extension to Brooklyn was begun the following year.

Elevated railroad spur from Third Avenue to Grand Central Depot
1878
Courtesy: The New-York Historical Society

Above:
Borough Hall, Brooklyn *circa*
1896-98
*Collection: The New-York Historical
Society*

Samuel H. Gottscho
American
**Luna Park, Coney Island,
Brooklyn, New York** 1906
Built 1903
*Collection: Museum of the City of
New York*

In an 1883 issue of *Harper's New
Monthly Magazine,* a journalist
predicted that the Bridge's rail cars
would play an important part in
getting New Yorkers to one of
their favorite spots for relaxation:
Coney Island. "These [cars] will
take [New Yorkers] across in a
little less than five minutes," the
journalist noted, "and it is not
improbable that through trains
will ultimately convey passengers
from the northernmost end of
New York, over the Brooklyn
Elevated that is to be, bringing
them nearer to the health-giving
beaches of Long Island by nearly
half an hour's time."

Right:
**"Born and Bred in Brooklyn" or
"Over the Bridge"**
Three pages of sheet music from
The Rise of Rosie O'Reilly, a 1922
musical comedy by George M.
Cohan
*Collection: Brian Rushton and Nancy
Reynolds, New York*

Below:
**Dodgers/Yankees World Series
Program** 1947
29.5 x 22.0 cm. (11⅞ x 8¾ in.)
*Collection: The Long Island Historical
Society, New York*

Facing page:
Brooklyn Bridge postcards
Private Collection, New York

104

BROOKLYN BRIDGE, N.Y. CITY.

S. Brooklyn Bridge, N.Y.

HARTFORD BRIDGE

Brooklyn Bridge.

Brooklyn Bridge, New York.

15. Brooklyn Bridge, New York.

Brooklyn Bridge, New York.

Brooklyn Bridge, New York.

IRVING UNDERHILL

Brooklyn Bridge and New York Skyline.

Brooklyn Bridge at Night
New York

The Cables, Brooklyn Bridge, New York.

View from Brooklyn Bridge Tower, New York.

Brooklyn Bridge from Brooklyn
New York City

BROOKLYN BRIDGE AND NEW YORK SKYLINE AT NIGHT.

Brooklyn and Manhattan Bridges, New York.

THE ROEBLING WORKS.
Every building shown above is used in the manufacture of Wire Rope or Wire.

JOHN A. ROEBLING'S SONS COMPANY, Trenton, N. J.
AGENCIES AND BRANCHES: New York, Chicago, Cleveland, Philadelphia, San Francisco, Atlanta.

ROEBLING'S
Steel and Iron

Of Every Kind and for Every Purpose. **Suspension Bridge Cables a Specialty.**

Covington and Cincinnati Suspension Bridge, built by John A. Roebling. Main Span 1,057 feet.

Pulleys and Ropes for the Transmission of Power Long Distances.

Manufacturers of Charcoal and Swedes Iron, Bessemer and Crucible Steel Wires.

GALVANIZED TELEGRAPH WIRE A SPECIALTY.

Works and Office,   Branch Office,   Office and Warehouse,
Trenton, N.J.   14 Drum St., San Francisco.   117 & 119 Liberty St., N.Y.

H. L. SHIPPY, Agent.

When transportation problems forced John Roebling to consider relocating his wire-rope business from Saxonburg, Pennsylvania, Peter Cooper, the builder of America's first locomotive, proposed Trenton, New Jersey, as a desirable location. Although Trenton was still a small town, it was well situated, with water and rail transport, skilled labor, and related industry nearby. In August 1848, Roebling purchased twenty-five acres at Trenton adjacent to canal and railway lines. The following year he moved his entire business there and began manufacturing both wire and cable. All of the buildings and machinery were designed by Roebling himself. The Trenton works—which included mills, furnaces, and laboratories—grew to employ almost 8,000 persons manufacturing every imaginable wire product from hairpins to harbor-defense nets.

At the turn of the century the need for specialty steel for new wire products made a large new plant of urgent importance to the Roebling company. In 1904, Charles Roebling, the third son of John Roebling and a masterful builder of the Roebling business after his father's death, built a giant steel plant near Kinkora, New Jersey. Since there was no local housing, a new town called Roebling was built. The houses were of varying character—larger ones for management, smaller ones for laborers. About 750 families were settled there by 1930.

Williamsburg Bridge

Left:
Williamsburg Bridge
Completed 1903
From Hamilton Schuyler,
The Roeblings, 1931

Below left:
Manhattan Bridge
Completed 1909
From Hamilton Schuyler,
The Roeblings, 1931

Below:
George Washington Bridge under construction n.d.
Completed 1931
Courtesy: Columbia University, New York

Manhattan Bridge

Roebling wire has been used in many of the most important suspension bridges built in the United States in the twentieth century. Among them are three New York bridges: the Williamsburg Bridge, the Manhattan Bridge, and the George Washington Bridge.

Left:
Letterhead of John A. Roebling's Sons Company 1895
Collection: Rutgers University, New Jersey

107

"The wonder and the triumph of this work of our own day is in the weaving of the aerial span that carries such burden of usefulness by human thought and skill, from the delicate threads of wire that a child could almost sever."

The Bridge has inspired countless artists, writers, and poets since these lines were written by a journalist of 1883. One thinks immediately of such masterpieces as the famous Hart Crane poem "To Brooklyn Bridge" (published in 1930 with photographs by Walker Evans). The works illustrated on the following pages briefly survey this rich artistic history (see also Lewis Kachur's essay "The Bridge as Icon").

Joseph Pennell
American, 1860-1926
Brooklyn Bridge n.d.
Watercolor and Conte crayon on paper
33.0 × 24.1 cm.
(13 × 9½ in.) sight
Collection: Mr. and Mrs. Jerome B. Weinstein, Pennsylvania

Albert Gleizes
French, 1881-1953
Brooklyn Bridge 1915
Oil on canvas
101.9 × 101.9 cm.
(40⅛ × 40⅛ in.)
Collection: The Solomon R. Guggenheim Museum, New York

Above:
Rudolph Ruzicka
American, 1883-1978
Brooklyn Bridge *circa* 1915
Wood engraving
Image: 18.8 × 17.6 cm. (7⅜ × 6⅞ in.)
Collection: The Brooklyn Museum, New York
Gift of the artist

Top right:
Louis Lozowick
American, 1892-1973
New York 1923
Lithograph
Image: 29.2 × 22.9 cm. (11½ × 9 in.)
Collection: Mr. and Mrs. Jacob Kainen, Maryland

Right:
Frederick T. Weber
American, 1883-1956
Peck Slip, New York *circa* 1930
Etching
Image: 22.4 × 30.0 cm.
(8⅞ × 11¾ in.)
Collection: The Brooklyn Museum, New York

Karl Zerbe
American, 1903-1972
Brooklyn Bridge *circa* 1946
Encaustic on canvas
92.7 × 101.9 cm.
(36½ × 40⅛ in.)
Collection: The Newark Museum,
New Jersey

Reginald Marsh
American, 1898-1954
Two Life Boats and the
Brooklyn Bridge n.d.
Watercolor on paper
35.6 × 50.8 cm.
(14 × 20 in.)
Collection: Marbella Gallery,
New York

Joseph Stella
American, 1877-1946
Study for New York Interpreted
circa 1920
Watercolor and gouache on paper
27.3 × 50.2 cm.
(10¾ × 19¾ in.)
Collection:
Yale University Art Gallery,
Connecticut
Gift of the Estate of
Katherine S. Dreier

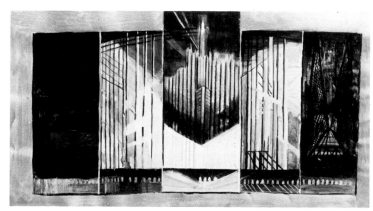

Bernice Abbott
American, b. 1898
**Brooklyn Bridge, Pier 21,
Pennsylvania Railroad**
March 30, 1937
Silver gelatin print
20.3 × 25.4 cm. (8 × 10 in.)
Collection:
Museum of the City of New York

Andreas Feininger
American, b. 1906
Above left:
New York: East River, Brooklyn and Manhattan Bridges 1940
Silver gelatin print
27.9 × 35.6 cm. (11 × 14 in.)
Copyright Andreas Feininger
Courtesy: Daniel Wolf, Inc., New York

Above right:
**New York: Downtown Manhattan and Brooklyn Bridge
Seen from Manhattan Bridge** 1940
Silver gelatin print
27.9 × 35.6 cm. (11 × 14 in.)
Copyright Andreas Feininger
Courtesy: Daniel Wolf, Inc., New York

113

Andreas Feininger
American, b. 1906
New York: The Underside of Brooklyn Bridge 1940
Silver gelatin print; 25.4 × 20.3 cm. (10 × 8 in.)
Copyright Andreas Feininger
Collection: Daniel Wolf, Inc., New York

Esther Bubley
American, b. 1921

Above left:
**Painters at Work on the
Brooklyn Bridge** 1946
Silver gelatin print
26.7 × 26.7 cm. (10½ × 10½ in.)
Collection:
*The Brooklyn Museum, New York
Gift of Standard Oil Co.*

Above right:
**From the Footpath on the
Brooklyn Bridge, New York Harbor
Looking towards Manhattan** n.d.
Silver gelatin print
24.1 × 34.3 cm. (9½ × 13½ in.)
Collection:
*The Brooklyn Museum, New York
Gift of Standard Oil Co.*

Left:
Erich Hartmann
American, b. 1922
**Sunday under the Bridge
Abandoned Car** August 1955
Silver gelatin print
19.7 × 27.3 cm. (7¾ × 10¾ in.)
Collection: Grace M. Mayer,
New York

Erich Hartmann
American, b. 1922

Above:
**Sunday under the Bridge
(The Bridge and Dover Street)**
August 1955
Silver gelatin print
33.3 × 46.0 cm.
(13⅛ × 18⅛ in.)
Collection:
Grace M. Mayer, New York

Top right:
**Sunday under the Bridge
(Fulton and Front Streets)**
August 1955
Silver gelatin print
33.3 × 23.5 cm.
(13⅛ × 9¼ in.)
Collection:
Grace M. Mayer, New York

Right:
Sunday under the Bridge
August 1955
Silver gelatin print
35.6 × 27.9 cm.
(14 × 11 in.)
Collection: The artist,
Magnum Photos, New York

Left:
Antonio Frasconi
American, b. 1919
Proem: To Brooklyn Bridge n.d.
Woodcut, 3 sheets
186.1 × 41.9 cm.
(73¼ × 16½ in.) sight
Collection:
The Brooklyn Museum, New York

Above:
Lyonel Feininger
American, 1871-1956
Untitled 1954
Pencil on paper
Dimensions not known
Collection:
Estate of the artist

117

Milton Bond
American, b. 1918
Brooklyn Bridge in 1914 1981
Painting on glass
40.6 × 50.8 cm.
(16 × 20 in.)
Collection:
America's Folk Heritage
Gallery, New York

Above:
George Comptis
American, b. 1934
Brooklyn Bridge No. 4 1969
Oil on canvas
167.6 × 137.2 cm.
(66 × 54 in.)
Collection:
Raymond K. Price, Jr., New York

Right:
Ellsworth Kelly
American, b. 1923
Brooklyn Bridge IV 1956-58
Oil on canvas
76.2 × 33.0 cm.
(30 × 13 in.)
Collection:
Dr. and Mrs. Sheldon Krasnow,
Illinois

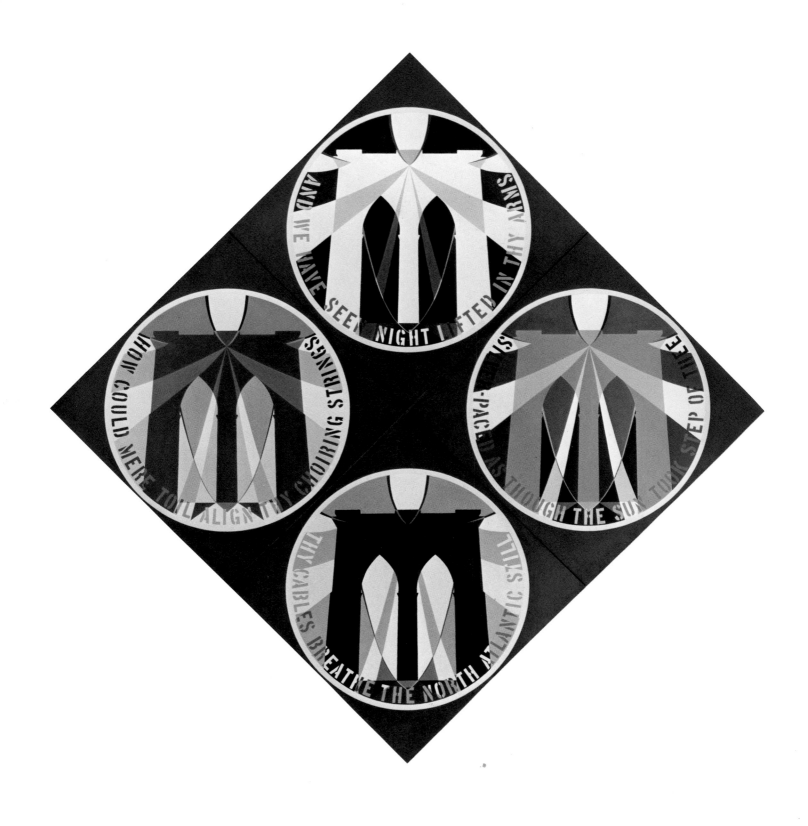

Robert Indiana
American, b. 1928
The Brooklyn Bridge 1964
Oil on canvas
Four panels, each 121.9 × 121.9 cm.
(48 × 48 in.)
Collection:
The Detroit Institute of Arts, Michigan
Founders Society Purchase,
Mr. and Mrs. Walter B. Ford II Fund

Left:
Karen Riedener
American, b. 1946
Brooklyn Bridge 1982
Silver gelatin photographic construction
121.9 × 25.4 cm. (48 × 10 in.)
Collection: Bertha Urdang Gallery, New York

Above:
Richard Benson
American, b. 1943
Brooklyn Bridge 1981
Platinum/palladium print
26.0 × 43.2 cm. (10¼ × 17 in.)
Collection: Washburn Gallery, New York

Above:
Arthur Cohen
American, b. 1928
Brooklyn Bridge No. 8 1982
Etching and aquatint
Image: 22.5 × 37.5 cm. (8⅞ × 14¾ in.)
Collection: The Brooklyn Museum, New York
Gift of the artist

Chronology

Barbara Head Millstein

1802 **February 18:** The New York *Evening Post* publishes a petition to the State Legislature by citizens of Manhattan and Long Island citing the need for a bridge between the two islands. The proposal raises much dispute as to the method of constructing a bridge which would not impede shipping on the East River.

1807 **February 28:** John Stevens, a noted inventor, petitions the State Senate concerning a system of floating bridges to span the Hudson and East Rivers. He later advocates tunnels and permanent bridges, but his proposed designs arouse such opposition on the grounds that they would obstruct navigation that his petition is denied.

1809 **February 13:** Thomas Pope, a carpenter-architect, invites the New York Common Council to see a model of his "Flying Pendent Lever Bridge." The plan calls for a single 1,800-foot span soaring 223 feet above the East River, connecting Fulton Street in New York with Fulton Street in Brooklyn. Pope also called it his "rainbow bridge" and described it in *A Treatise on Bridge Architecture* published in 1811.

1829 **November 5:** A project to build a bridge from the foot of Maiden Lane in Brooklyn, high enough to allow the largest ships to pass under it, is reported in the New York *Gazette and General Advertiser.* The estimated cost is given as $600,000.

1845 Nathaniel S. Prime, in a *History of Long Island*, records that although a bridge between New York and Brooklyn had been "the great topic of conversation" in the early 1800s, by "now the idea of a bridge is as rare a conception as a 'fifth wheel to a coach,' and is about as desirable."

1857 **April 4:** *Harper's Weekly* announces that "a bill is before the Legislature to throw a suspension bridge over the East River from New York to Brooklyn...The plan is pronounced feasible and within the cost of a profitable invention, by Mr. [John] Roebling, the architect of the Niagra suspension bridge."

1865 John A. Roebling, with the assistance of Wilhelm Hildenbrand, prepares a set of plans for his bridge.

1866 **December 21:** At a conference in Brooklyn, State Senator Henry Cruse Murphy, contractor William C. Kingsley, and Judge Alexander McCue reach an agreement that results in the passage of an act by the New York State Legislature (April 16, 1867) providing for the construction of the New York and Brooklyn Bridge. Under the Enabling Act, Brooklyn puts up three million dollars in capital stock; New York contributes only half as much.

1867 **April 16:** The New York Bridge Company is incorporated.

May 23: The New York Bridge Company appoints John Augustus Roebling chief engineer in charge of construction.

Facing page:
Richard Haas
American, b. 1936
Mural at South Street, Peck Slip
1978
Exterior enamel paint
13.72 x 27.44 meters (45 x 90 feet)
Photo: Donna Svennevik
Courtesy: Public Art Fund, Inc., New York

1867   **September 1:** In a forty-eight page report entitled *To the President and Directors of the New York Bridge Company on the Proposed East River Bridge* Roebling discusses his system of trussing and inclined stays running diagonally from the Bridge tower. He claims that if the proposed four main cables were removed, the Bridge would sink but the trussing and stays would keep it from falling. Despite public and professional incredulity, the plan is subsequently approved.

1869   **June 21:** The Secretary of War officially informs the Bridge Company that he has approved the plan and location of the Bridge. President Ulysses S. Grant subsequently signs a Federal bill passed by Congress to the same effect.

July 22: John A. Roebling dies at the age of sixty-three as the result of an accident that occurred when he was making observations to determine the exact location of the Brooklyn tower. His son, Col. Washington Roebling, is appointed to succeed him as Chief Engineer.

1870   **January 3:** Work on the Bridge begins with the tearing out of the spare slips of the Fulton Ferry in preparation for the foundations of the Brooklyn tower.

March 19: The caisson for the Brooklyn tower, built by the engineering firm of Webb and Bell, is launched and towed into position. On June 16, the first blocks of granite are laid on the caisson while excavation continues underneath it. The caisson is finally filled and finished on March 11, 1871.

September 15: The city begins buying land for the Manhattan end of the Bridge, a process that continues until 1896. Final settlement appears not to have been made until well into the 1930s.

December 2: Fire in the Brooklyn caisson necessitates flooding of the caisson, delaying progress for almost three months and costing $15,000. Col. Roebling and six other men are stricken by "caisson disease."

1871   **May 18:** The New York caisson is launched (and is filled and finished by May 1872). Although the Brooklyn caisson hit bedrock at 44½ feet, the foundation on the New York side rests on tightly packed sand at 78½ feet. One hundred ten men on the New York side were stricken with caisson disease.

1872   During the summer, Col. Roebling is stricken once more by caisson disease, becoming a nearly helpless invalid and suffering the aftereffects for the rest of his life. From this time on he directs the building of the Bridge from his sickroom, with his wife Emily delivering his orders to the Bridge engineers.

1874   **June 5:** An act is passed authorizing New York and Brooklyn to assume control of the Brooklyn Bridge while repaying the original subscribers with interest. The Bridge is placed under the management of a board of trustees, ten from each city including both mayors and comptrollers. Brooklyn is to raise two thirds of the funds; New York one third. The bridge thus becomes a public work.

1875   **May:** The Brooklyn tower is completed.

1876   **July:** The New York tower is completed.

August 14: Master mechanic E. F. Farrington makes the first trip between the towers riding in a boatswain's chair attached to the traveler wire.

1877   **February 9:** A temporary footbridge between the towers is completed and crossed.

May 29: The first cable wire is drawn across the river.

1878   **October 5:** The last wire is drawn across the river.

November: Lack of funds causes the first of a number of interruptions in the work. News breaks of a scandal over the supply of faulty wire.

1879   Work commences on the building of the approaches to the bridge.

1882   **June 29:** The Legislature directs that the cities of New York and Brooklyn pay to the trustees of the Brooklyn Bridge the sum of $1.25 million "or so much thereof as shall be necessary to complete the Bridge in the proportion of one third from New York and two thirds from Brooklyn."

1883   **May 24:** The Brooklyn Bridge is formally opened and dedicated. During the course of its construction approximately twenty-seven men had lost their lives, including John A. Roebling. In his speech, Congressman Abram S. Hewitt, later elected mayor of New York, says: "When we turn to the graceful structure at whose portals we stand, and when the airy outline of its curves and beauty, pendent between massive towers suggestive of art alone, is contrasted with the over-reaching vault of heaven above and the ever-moving flood of waters beneath we are irresistibly moved to exclaim, 'What hath *man* wrought!'"

1883 **May 30:** Decoration Day. Ten thousand holiday sightseers and fifteen members of Company A of the 12th Regiment are on the Bridge when a woman slips and falls on the steps leading to the Bridge turnstiles. When the ensuing panic and stampede is over, twelve persons, including two children, are dead. This is the first and last major tragedy on the Bridge.

September: Cable cars are installed, running on both sides of the promenade next to the roadways. A ride costs a nickel. Other tolls include ten cents for a wagon drawn by one horse (twenty cents if drawn by two horses); two cents apiece for sheep and hogs; and three cents for bicycles.

1888 The electric lights on the Bridge are declared by the Lighthouse Board to be a menace to river navigation. The problem is corrected by equipping them with reflectors.

1891 Tolls for pedestrians are abolished.

1892 A record crowd of almost a quarter of a million people crosses the bridge on Columbus Day, the four hundredth anniversary of the "discovery" of America.

1893 In order to encourage the "noble art of cycling," the toll for bicycles is reduced to a penny. But cyclists raise such a fuss at having to dismount to pay *any* toll that, in 1894, it too is abolished.

1896 **February 7:** The Bridge rides out a 72-mile-per-hour gale, dispersing all misgivings about its ability to withstand windstorms. No subsequent wind has affected its structure.

1898 **January 1:** Brooklyn becomes a borough of New York City.

Electric trolleys come into service on the Bridge. With their tracks laid on the roadways, traffic on each roadway is squeezed into one lane instead of two. Electric trains of the Brooklyn Elevated Company are also introduced, replacing the cable cars except during rush hours when both kinds of train run on the same tracks (the "Els" using the cable mechanism at rush hours, and electricity at other times).

July 29: At six o'clock in the evening a traffic jam near the Brooklyn end of the Bridge ties up wagons and trolleys all the way back to the Manhattan entrance. Suddenly the Bridge sags a few inches at two points, approximately 250 feet on both sides of the Manhattan tower. On examination, engineers find that several trusses buckled under the roadbed, but they conclude that the damage is harmless, and make no attempt to straighten the kinks. For a few days after the incident the ferries running across the river (eleven now compared with the fourteen that had existed during the building of the Bridge) do a brisk business.

1901 **July 24:** Several of the suspender rods near the center of the main span snap because of heat expansion. It is discovered that the joints connecting them to the Bridge's deck lacked "give" because they had not been recently oiled. The rods are pronounced sound by the Bridge engineers, but those nearest the center of the Bridge are replaced with larger ones and the joints are kept oiled.

1903 **December 12:** Commissioner Gustave Lindenthal of the Department of Bridges proposes to New York Mayor Seth Low that steadily growing traffic on the Brooklyn Bridge indicates a need for an extra deck and two extra trains that, in turn, would require the installation of another set of cables, stays, and suspenders half way up the towers. The plan is abandoned as too expensive, but the traffic problem continues to grow.

December 19: The Williamsburg Bridge to Brooklyn (Lefferts Buck, Engineer) opens. It does little to ease traffic on the Brooklyn Bridge.

1907 Estimates show that half a million people cross the Brooklyn Bridge on an average day.

1908 The cable cars are removed, but additional coaches are added to the elevated trains and the tracks are heavily reinforced, increasing the load on the Bridge. The South Ferry station on the Lexington Avenue subway comes into service.

1909 **December 31:** The Manhattan Bridge to Brooklyn (Gustave Lindenthal, engineer) opens. For a short time, traffic on the Brooklyn Bridge is relieved.

1915 The New York City Board of Aldermen changes the Bridge's name from the New York and Brooklyn Bridge to the Brooklyn Bridge. The subways begin to run beneath the East River, starting with the I.R.T. line from 42nd Street.

1920 The Seventh Avenue subway at Old Slip (built in 1919), and the B.M.T. line at Whitehall Street and 60th Street, tunnel under the river, but the traffic on the Bridge is between six and eight times heavier than it was when the Bridge opened.

1922 **July 3:** It is discovered that the two northernmost cables have slightly shifted at the point where they cross the Manhattan tower. The eleven saddles that support the cables have been dragged a little towards the center of the Bridge, and the rollers on which the saddles rest have become rigid with rust, endangering the cables' ability to adjust to changes in weight.

1922   **July 6:** All motor traffic is barred from the Bridge. Trains are ordered to keep a thousand feet apart, and trolleys a hundred feet, while crossing the Bridge. Grover Whalen, Commissioner of Plants and Structures under New York Mayor John F. Hylan, proposes that the Bridge be rebuilt. Gustave Lindenthal (engineer of the Manhattan Bridge) says there is no danger, and Washington Roebling (now eighty-five and living in retirement in Trenton, New Jersey) agrees, saying, "The Bridge is good for another century." The cables, it turns out, had been designed to slip, and their slipping showed that they were automatically equalizing the load. When the cables ceased moving, fear abated. But the Bridge remained closed except to mass transit and pedestrians.

1925   **May:** The Bridge is reopened to automobile traffic, but trucks—except for those used for mail and newspaper deliveries—remain banned.

1929   The *SS America* is forced to cut thirty feet off its top mast in order to pass under the Bridge and reach its berth in drydock.

1931   New York Mayor Jimmy Walker receives a note threatening to blow up the Brooklyn Bridge. The note is signed with what appears to be the initials "KKK."

1935   The *Engineering News-Record* refers to the Bridge as "hardly more than a sentimental landmark."

1942   **June 30:** The ferry to Greenpoint, Brooklyn—the last East River ferry in service—goes out of business.

1944   The Bridge's elevated trains are discontinued.

1945   The Bridge stations and the William Street footbridge to City Hall Park are removed.

1946   After a two-year inspection, a team of bridge engineers concludes that all the Bridge requires is a coat of paint.

1949   The Steinman Company is given the job of rehabilitating the Bridge. The work involves taking up the trolley and "el" tracks and the trusses that separate them from the roadways; widening the two roadways to thirty-foot, three-lane highways; replacing the old roadways with steel mesh and concrete; and laying a new wooden floor on the promenade.

1950   The cost of remodeling the Bridge is estimated at about $7 million.

January 22: In order to take measurements to determine the exact vertical curve of the Bridge, engineers bring about the first total closing of the Bridge (8:00 A.M. to 3:55 P.M.) in its history.

March 6: Remodeling work begins on the Bridge, and the trolley makes its last run from Manhattan's Park Row to Brooklyn. The 104 passengers included a Brooklyn couple who had used the trolley for fifty years, an elderly gentleman who had first ridden over in 1898, and a Boy Scout who blew taps.

1952   Three lanes of auto traffic in both directions come into operation, and all truck traffic is eliminated.

1981   As a precautionary measure, work commences on a project to strengthen the main cables at the anchorages by forcing liquid zinc into the miniscule space surrounding the wires where they meet the anchor. The work is to be completed by 1983. Although a pedestrian is killed in June when a diagonal stay snaps, there appears to be general agreement that the Bridge is good for another hundred years.

The Builders

People in modern times are so familiar with large and exact achievements in practical science that they are apt to forget the processes by which those achievements are accomplished.

THOMAS KINSELLA
in the Brooklyn *Eagle*, 1872

David McCullough

They are all gone now, every one—the Roeblings and the assistant engineers Collingwood, Paine, Probasco, Hildenbrand, McNulty, C. C. Martin; and the Brooklyn contractor, plain, blunt William Kingsley, who started things rolling and lined his pockets nowhere near so well as he might have; and "Boss" Tweed and "Brains" Sweeny, who had an "understanding" with Kingsley and might have made a fortune had the Ring not collapsed in 1871, only two years after the work was under way; and State Senator Henry Cruse Murphy, the very essence of "Old Brooklyn," and Abram Hewitt and Teddy Roosevelt's black-sheep uncle, Robert, and the

George W. Pach
American
Brooklyn Bridge Under Construction: President, Treasurer, Engineers and Foremen October 1878 *(detail)*
Silver gelatin print
Collection:
Museum of the City of New York

Taken on top of the Brooklyn anchorage at the point where the cables tie into the anchor bars, this photograph shows State Senator Henry Cruse Murphy (center, with arms folded) talking to some of Roebling's assistant engineers. The man wearing the high silk hat in the right foreground is probably George McNulty. William Paine is seated (center) looking directly into the camera. Fifth from the left in the group standing by the wooden structure is Wilhelm Hildenbrand. Master mechanic E. F. Farrington is sixth from the left, and Roebling's second-in-command, C. C. Martin, seventh.

127

No public work of importance could be built in New York without the approval of **William Marcy Tweed,** head of Tammany Hall. Until his infamous "Ring" fell in 1871, Tweed and his "associates" used the Bridge to provide jobs for their friends and to line their own pockets.

Democrat **Abram Hewitt,** known for his moral rectitude and later role as mayor of New York, was both a member of the Bridge board and the secret financial backer of J. Lloyd Haigh, the Brooklyn wire manufacturer who defrauded the Bridge Company.

bright, scrubbed "Boy Mayor" of Brooklyn, Seth Low, all of whom served on the board; and Kinsella of the *Eagle,* who stood behind the work from beginning to end; and J. Lloyd Haigh, the shadowy wire manufacturer from South Brooklyn who wound up in Sing Sing for his efforts.

Some are known more for what they did in later years, like Hewitt, who became mayor of New York; or Dr. Walter Reed, who was then an intern at Brooklyn City Hospital looking after the men brought in with the bends; or an English laborer named Frank Harris, who wrote a sensational pornographic book, *My Lifes and Loves.* But so memorable a figure as E. F. Farrington, the "master mechanic," the one who blew kisses to the crowds as he sailed over the East River the summer of 1876, riding the first wire strung between the towers, fades from the record from the time the work ended. We don't know what became of him. Or of so many others: the stonemasons, carpenters, riggers, machinists, blacksmiths, riveters, and all those ordinary day laborers who went into the terrifying caissons beneath the river for such bonanza wages as two dollars a day.

Only a relative handful even have names now. Mike Lynch remains a known quantity because he is said to have been "the first Irishman" to go into the Brooklyn caisson and the last to come out; and we know of a watchman named Al Smith, because his son and namesake became governor. The other names, the few scraps of personal information available, are mainly from reports on the ones who were killed.

All told, several thousand people took part over fourteen years, many who were American born (including some blacks), many Germans, some Italians, some English, at least one Chinese, and a great many Irish. They all worked a ten-hour day, six days a week, and they were all men—with the one exception of Emily Roebling.

The last of them died in January 1980, in a home for the elderly in Harlem, at the age of 106. He was Henry Jones; he had been a waterboy during the final part of the work in 1882 or '83, which would have made him eight or nine at the time.

Even the spectators are gone now. Governor Al Smith, who grew up on South Street, "in the shadow of the New York tower," loved to describe the spectacle of workers scrambling high up among the cables. When he was eight or nine, his father took him across the temporary catwalk, while his mother stayed home, sitting in her chair, saying her rosary over and over the whole time they were gone. It was his mother who told him of the horrifying work in the caissons. "Perhaps had they known," she would say, "they never would have built it."

But build it they did, calling it a variety of names—the East River Bridge, the New York Bridge, the Brooklyn Bridge, the Roebling Bridge, the Great Bridge, or merely the Bridge—and to anyone who knows what they went through, it can never be thought of as just an engineering marvel, or an architectural masterpiece, or the perfect expression of nineteenth-century industrialism, or a turning point in urban American history, or a nice way to go over the river. It is, besides all that, their story.

It was conceived in winter, in the mind of John Augustus Roebling, the illustrious pioneer builder of suspension bridges and wealthy wire manufacturer of Trenton, New Jersey. According to the accepted account, he was caught in the ice on a Brooklyn ferry and "then and there," scanning the distance between shores, envisioned his crowning work. His oldest son, Washington, age fifteen, happened also to be with him at the time.

That was in 1852, thirty years before the fact. It was not until after the Civil War and after the opening of the celebrated Roebling bridge at Cincinnati (which still stands) that William Kingsley went to Trenton to talk about building one at Brooklyn. Kingsley had no specific kind of bridge in mind.

No one in Brooklyn did, apparently. It was the man they wanted, not a particular plan—which is fascinating, since the man was exactly what they were not to have.

His brilliance was well established. His abiding confidence in science, as all of science and technology were known, was in perfect harmony with the very Jules Verne outlook of the times. "It will no longer suit the spirit of the present age to pronounce an undertaking impracticable," Roebling had written. A German by birth, he had been trained at the Polytechnic Institute in Berlin. He was the first to manufacture wire rope, or cable, in America; the first to perfect a suspension, or wire-hung bridge that could carry a railroad (at Niagara Falls); the first to dare anything even approaching the size and weight of the one at Cincinnati. He was a technical virtuoso, designer, mathematician, inventor, industrial entrepreneur, a success at everything he put his mind to.

Further, his bridges were thrilling to see, as his Brooklyn clients found for themselves on the tour he led cross-country to Cincinnati and Niagara Falls in the spring of 1869. They could count on a triumph of art no less than advanced engineering, he assured them, and to judge by his photograph the look in the pale, intense eyes must have been something.

In appearance, in manner, he was above the crowd, all business. Once, on a call to Washington, D.C., during the Civil War, he scrawled a note on the back of his card and sent it in to General John Charles Frémont: "Sir. You are keeping me waiting. John Roebling has not the leisure to wait on any man."

Anonymous
John Augustus Roebling *circa* 1866
(detail)
Silver gelatin print
*Collection: The Brooklyn Museum,
New York*

There is more, however, and it, too, bears on the story. We don't know everything by any means, which is a shame, since we can never know enough about genius, but in unpublished family correspondence and his own journals, he emerges as a figure of strange, sometimes violent lights and shadows. He was cold, vain, and suspicious, a man tormented by insomnia, bad digestion, spells of terrible self-recrimination. He plunged into spiritualism, became a fanatic—there is no other word for it—on hydropathy, the water cure. His children, for whom he had little time, were terrified of him. "Brutal" is a word Washington Roebling used to describe him.

An unforgettable vignette has come down through the family. John A. Roebling stands outside the Trenton mill where a number of donkeys are used to drag heavy strands of wire through long beds of sand, as part of the finishing process. One of the animals dallies or strays from the prescribed path, and John A. Roebling walks up, takes it by the head, and breaks its neck.

When the youngest of his children, Edmund, misbehaved in some unknown fashion, Roebling very nearly beat him to death. The boy ran off, disappeared, and was later found in a Philadelphia jail where, according to Washington, he had had himself entered as a common vagrant "and . . . was enjoying life for the first time."

"The hero is admired and proclaimed a public benefaction," Roebling himself wrote in private. " . . . But nobody knows. . . . Who can hide me from myself?"

The heaviest blow he inflicted on Washington was his own hideous death just as the real work at Brooklyn was about to begin. There was a foolish accident. Roebling was standing beside the ferry slip, helping with the surveys and with such concentration that when the boat docked he neglected to get out of the way. The boat jammed against a stringpiece which caught and crushed his foot. Washington was with him at the time, and later, when he had several of his toes amputated (without anesthetic at his wish), and later still through the gruesome, final agonies of lockjaw. Roebling had dismissed the doctors, insisting that water, poured steadily on the open wound, was the one and only cure.

The bridge he had projected on paper was to surpass any on earth in size, cost, and "audacity." Two stupendous gothic towers, larger than anything on either skyline, were to reach 270 feet in the air, and four great cables would carry the roadway, or deck, more than a hundred feet above the river, high enough so all but the largest of the clipper ships could pass below without trimming their top gallants. An unprecedented $7 million was at stake, he had estimated, not to mention the reputations of his clients. But as of the morning of July 22, 1869, he was dead, and with Washington the only one around who knew enough to carry on, the others—Kingsley, Murphy—saw no choice but to put him in charge at once.

The Colonel, as they called him, was then all of thirty-two years old. He had only the most preliminary plans at hand, as he later acknowledged, no working drawings, "nothing fixed or decided." All he really had to go by were his wits, experience, and "vitality," a favorite Roebling word. He was married and the father of one child, a little boy whom his wife had chosen to name John A. Roebling II. His salary was handsome, $10,000 a year, but his expenses would run beyond that, so financially the Bridge was to mean no profit for him, not a dollar in fourteen years.

It was the understanding since boyhood that he must follow in his father's path, he being the oldest son. He had been sent to the Rensselaer Polytechnic Institute at Troy, New York, in 1854, then, four years later, to Pittsburgh to begin his apprenticeship working on a bridge of his father's over the Allegheny River. After the war, he was dispatched to Cincinnati to become his father's first assistant. With the Cincinnati Bridge completed, he was off to Europe with his bride for nearly a year to study the use of pneumatic caissons in advance of the work at Brooklyn. Other, younger sons were kept at home, meantime, consigned to the prospering family business.

He never reported to anyone but his father; he was forever being judged by his father. The war was the single interruption, but even then it was his father, one highly unpleasant evening at the dinner table, who ordered him out of the house and into the army. The father despised slavery, so the son had to march with Mr. Lincoln's army.

In some ways they were alike. The elder man played the flute and piano, the younger man the violin. Washington could "make a violin talk," we read in a letter from a friend. He had his father's extraordinary physical stamina, his father's steadfastness in the face of adversity. He had been raised on an unyielding Germanic pride in one's work, on duty and cold baths in the morning. But he also had a lovely, wry sense of humor. He was soft-spoken, informal, modest to a fault some thought. He deplored vanity as the most costly of human follies. History, he had decided, favored the vain, and he had little faith in history. He was drawn to astronomy and botany, was particularly strong in geology, and had begun what would become one of the finest mineral collections in the country, if not the world. He adored Goethe (in the original German), chess, opera, roses, a good cigar, the absolute dark of night out of doors, and architecture. Architecture, he came to believe, was the "noblest" art. He drew beautifully. His mind was not the creative engine his father's had been, but he was exceptionally observant and retentive, and could improvise with speed and ingenuity, a gift prized among American engineers of his generation.

The biggest experience of his life until Brooklyn was the war—and in many ways it is the key to the man and what he did at Brooklyn. He had been through "any quantity of hard fighting," from Manassas Junction to Antietam to Gettysburg to the Wilderness to the siege of Petersburg. Miraculously he survived—at Antietam a cannonball came so close it sucked the air out of his lungs—and he came out a brevet colonel, having enlisted as a private the day after his father ordered him from the house. He also built several successful bridges of his own, not his father's design, fell very much in love, and from watching some of the Union Army's most celebrated figures at close range (Hooker, Meade, Grant) formed decided views on what qualities counted most in a leader. Courage was essential. So was a level head and a reserve of strength for emergencies. So was "the intuitive faculty of being at the vital spot at the right time."

Many people were struck by what seemed an air of imperturbable calm about him. A fellow officer observing him during the siege of Petersburg described him as "a light-haired, blue-eyed man with a countenance as if all the world were an empty show." Washington himself said his eyes were green and confided to his future wife, Emily Warren, sister of his commanding officer, General G. K. Warren, that in truth he worried about almost everything.

He took charge without a moment's hesitation, knowing as did nobody else how much his father had left unresolved, and knowing that unlike his father he had no one standing by should something happen to him.

The able and, as it turned out, exceedingly loyal staff he assembled were nearly all younger even than he. Indeed, not the least of the arresting facts about the Brooklyn Bridge is that the average age of the engineers who undertook to build it was about thirty-one. All the magnificent drawings were executed under his direction—developed, more often than not, from his preliminary sketches, and subject always to his final approval. He ordered materials, wrote specifications. His lengthy annual reports to the trustees remain models of thoroughness and clarity. Along with everything else, he wrote very well.

The two giant pneumatic caissons were his supreme contribution, however, and a test of everything that was in him. They were the foundations upon which the towers would stand, or to put it another way, they were the part of the Bridge nobody would ever see and the part upon which everything depended. And they are still there, beneath the towers, beneath the river, exactly where he calculated they ought to go.

Readers of such publications as *Harper's Weekly* or *Scientific American* were asked to imagine a colossal, bottomless wooden box filled with compressed air (to keep the river out) and held in position on the riverbed by the tower being built on top. Inside the box were a hundred men or more digging away with picks and shovels. As their work progressed (around the clock), and as

A cut-away drawing of the caisson showing the air locks, the supply shafts, and the water shafts by which excavated material was removed during the caisson's descent without losing air pressure in the work chambers. *Harper's Weekly.*

FOUNDATION LINE

Four sketches by an artist who made the journey down into the Brooklyn caisson show *(top left)* formally dressed visitors passing through an air lock; *(top right)* the ladder connecting the air lock with the work area; *(above left)* workers splitting one of the many boulders encountered during the excavations; and *(above right)* men stirring up a pool beneath a water shaft in order to ease the operation of the clamshell scoop that dropped down the shaft. *New York Public Library.*

the tremendous weight of the tower increased steadily, the box was being forced ever so slowly deeper and deeper in the riverbed until finally it would rest on bedrock. The box was equipped with air locks, iron chambers with trap doors, so the men could come and go without loss of air pressure, and a system of water shafts, the ingenious means devised by Roebling for the removal of excavation. The dimensions of the Brooklyn caisson, the first to go down, were 102 by 168 feet.

Nothing came easily. Boulders jammed beneath the outer or cutting edge. The river came in. As the caisson sank deeper and air pressure within had to be increased, men started experiencing a strange ringing in the ears. Their voices had a thin, eerie sound, and the heat and humidity of the compressed air became almost intolerable. Work in such an atmosphere was exhausting beyond anyone's experience, and scary, to say the least. The only illumination was candlelight or limelight. When fire broke out in December 1870, it burned into the huge overhead timbers with such intensity, because of the compressed air, that it seemed impossible to put out. Newspapers carried headlines of "The Terrible Conflagration." Roebling was in the caisson, directing the fight, for more than twenty hours, knowing the whole time that the fire could eat into the roof like a cancer and weaken it to the point where the tremendous weight of the tower would come crashing through.

"Colonel W. A. Roebling has given the work his unremitting attention at all times," William Kingsley reported to the trustees, "but especially at all the critical points is he conspicuous for his presence and exertions. During the fire . . . when the destruction of the caisson was imminent, he remained in the caisson all night, putting forth almost superhuman efforts to extinguish it, and only came out when he supposed that the fire was extinguished, and when he felt the symptoms of paralysis . . . "

What he felt was the onset of the bends, or caisson disease, then still a mystery. In his determination to be always where he was needed, he customarily went in and out of the caisson more often in a day than anyone, and he was invariably, as we now know, coming out—out of the compressed air—far too rapidly. He was carried to his home on Brooklyn Heights and rubbed all over with a solution of salt and whiskey. Then, only an hour or two later, when a message arrived saying the fire had broken out again, he dressed and went back. His decision this time was to flood the caisson, something he dreaded doing. As it was, the tedious repairs of the fire set everything back three months.

They hit bedrock on the Brooklyn side at 44 feet 6 inches. On the New York side it was a different story, and the suffering from the bends there became alarming. Every two feet that the caisson descended meant another pound of pressure added to the air inside. As Roebling wrote, hardly anyone escaped without experiencing pain of the most intense kind—"like the thrust of a knife," said one worker. In April 1872, with the caisson at a depth of seventy-odd feet and still no bedrock, two men died. The strain for Roebling was nearly unbearable, as his wife later said. On May 18, a third man died, and that same day Roebling made the most difficult and courageous decision of the project. Staking everything—the success of the Bridge, his reputation, his career—he ordered a halt. The New York tower, he had concluded, could stand where it was, at a depth of 78 feet 6 inches, not on bedrock, but on "hardpack"—sand. From examinations of the strata he had determined to his own satisfaction that no movement had occurred at that level since the time of deposit millions of years in the geologic past; so, he said, it was "good enough to found upon." To have driven the caisson to bedrock, he estimated, might have taken another year, and possibly a hundred lives.

Sometime later, when he was seeing to the final details inside the caisson, before it was filled in with concrete, he suffered another collapse, this one far more serious, and from that point on he was to be seen no more. He became as the years passed the famous "man in the window," hidden away from everyone, unseen, but supposedly seeing all, running it all from his upstairs room.

Nowhere in the history of such great undertakings is there anything comparable. He directed every step of what was then the largest, most difficult engineering project ever attempted, with all its risks and complications, entirely in absentia. Nobody could see him except his doctors, a few chosen trustees, a few chosen subordinates, and his wife, and never more than one or two at a time. He was never known to go near the Bridge or to set foot on it in all the ten more years that the work continued. Only when the Bridge was finished would he reemerge, his health then, he acknowledged, much improved.

For about a year he was not even in Brooklyn, as supposed. He was running things from a sickroom in his father's house in Trenton. But in 1873 he returned to the house in Brooklyn, 110 Columbia Heights, with its sweeping panorama, and from then on the popular picture of the lone figure at his window, telescope or field glasses at hand, the Bridge in the distance, is accurate.

What was the matter with him? Why did he never come out of hiding? The common explanation was that he suffered complications resulting from his time in the caissons—from the bends, in other words. It was also rumored that he was out of his mind, and that if the truth were known his wife was in charge.

Those who did know never said much in explanation, but they also never referred to the bends or caisson disease by name. In a letter to his son years later, Roebling would recall being in such a state that he had to be fed. He was unable even to lift his arms, which may well have been a consequence of the bends. He also complained of failing vision, a symptom not associated with the disease, and for a considerable time was incapable of reading or writing anything.

Farrington, the master mechanic, a forthright, direct individual if ever there was one, said Roebling had become "a confirmed invalid . . . owing to exposure, overwork, and anxiety"—practically a textbook definition of what in that day was called neurasthenia, or nervous prostration. "He is not so sick as people imagine," Emily Roebling would explain when, in the final days of

the work, a single reporter was permitted into the house. His problem, she said, was an inability to endure people or their talk. Talk especially had a "very debilitating effect."

From his own later correspondence, now in a collection at Rutgers University, we know that a "course of electricity," or early, primitive electrical shock treatments, were tried, and they could only have been extremely painful. "Often the doctors said I could not live from day to day," he would write. For the rest of his life he would remember a summer heat wave in Brooklyn when he was "in bed" and the thermometer registered a hundred degrees or worse. He suffered unendingly, that much is certain. Recalling almost anything to do with the Bridge or Brooklyn, he would speak of "that fearful time," "that terrible burden," "the tortures I endured." "When I think of what I endured at Brooklyn, my heart sinks within me," he would write to his son.

It is also conceivable that he had become addicted to drugs, and this too may have had something to do with his self-inflicted seclusion. We know he

Master mechanic **E. F. Farrington** riding a boatswain's chair tied to an endless wire rope. This first crossing of the East River by way of the Bridge was made on August 25, 1876, and was watched by a crowd estimated at ten thousand. *Harper's New Monthly Magazine.*

was given morphine during the worst agonies of the bends and that morphine addiction as a consequence of just such situations was by no means uncommon. We know also that in later years, suffering from a variety of ills and pains, he relied rather heavily on laudanum, the most common narcotic of the day, and so there is little reason to suppose he did not do the same at Brooklyn. The one reporter who was allowed in at the end was struck by two things when taken in to see Roebling: the first was how well Roebling looked, the other was the "imposing array of medicine phials" to be seen on a side table. This could mean nothing at all or it could be that it was the reporter's way of raising suspicions in the minds of readers who were far more conversant with drugs and problems of addiction than many present-day readers appreciate.

Roebling's own explanation of his plight, expressed in a letter to one of his staff, was that he had pushed himself too far. Our very imprecise contemporary term would be a nervous breakdown. The remedy for "nervous diseases," he said, was to sit and keep quiet. Relief, if it came at all, could come "only through mental rest of all the faculties and especially the emotions." And while it is impossible to know just what he meant by the "emotions," it is also impossible not to wonder how much of his problem was psychosomatic in nature. He had made himself a prisoner in much the way his brother Edmund had, and perhaps for him too it meant freedom of a kind, perhaps the same freedom from his father, who could only have been an overpowering presence so long as the Bridge remained unfinished and his own duty to the great man's vision continued unfulfilled. Only in isolation could he hold on, keep his head. "I can only do my work by maintaining my independence," he told the trustees at one point.

Whatever the nature of his troubles, however mystifying his situation, his intellectual faculties suffered not at all. That he could keep everything in his head as he did is astonishing, like someone playing six games of chess at once blindfolded and winning them all. Nothing was done except as he specified. His was the single commanding intellect throughout, as his assistants were the first to acknowledge.

Also, most importantly, he had, as he put it, "a strong tower to lean upon, my wife, a woman of infinite tact and wisest counsel." She was tall, "strikingly English in style," with brown eyes and a cheerful, mobile expression. He wrote of how gracefully she moved, how entertaining she could be in conversation. "I think we will be a pair of lovers all our lifetime," he had written to her during the war, and from every indication we have, they were.

She became his private secretary, his nurse and constant companion, his means of contact with the trustees. She could talk to them, he said, as could no one else and with a conviction that carried much weight. When he was first stricken she had gone to Henry Cruse Murphy to explain the situation and was told things could continue as they were, with her husband in charge. She had expected his troubles would last only a short time.

She organized correspondence, kept his daily journal, and assisted in drafting specifications—mountainous tasks all in longhand. If the workers were his troops and he the commander on the hill, she was the trusted aide-de-camp, much as he had been for her brother in the war. If he was indispensable to the Bridge, she was indispensable to him. She went to the Bridge with his orders, or to be his "eyes," often several times a day and in all kinds of weather. By the final stages she was meeting with manufacturers to explain how certain parts had to be fabricated.

In the files of the Roebling Collection at the Rensselaer Polytechnic Institute there is a copy of a speech given by a graduate, a contemporary of Washington Roebling's, at a dinner in New York in 1882, the year before the Bridge was completed. Emily, we read, was a "woman of unusual executive ability. . . . She is firm and decided, with opinions on almost every subject

Anonymous
Emily Warren Roebling n.d.
Silver gelatin print
Collection: The Brooklyn Museum, New York

136

which opinions she expresses with great frankness. To her natural talents for organizing are found tact, energy, unselfishness and good nature . . . "

Progress on the Bridge all the while had come steadily, but slowly, in the face of one problem or frustration after another. Work was stalled by bad weather, financial crises, and labor troubles. Trustees complained of the delays. Spinning the cables was supposed to have been the smoothest part of the process, since the system had been perfected on earlier Roebling bridges, but then, in 1878, up popped J. Lloyd Haigh, the wire manufacturer, with his neat bit of deception. Had Roebling been on the job in person, it might never have happened. As it was he had warned the trustees in writing that Haigh was nobody to do business with and, further, if they did some checking they would find that Haigh was financially beholden to Abram Hewitt, the very member of the board who was doing the most to see that Haigh, not the Roebling company, got the contract.

The deception, once discovered, was painfully simple. Some of Roebling's own people had been stationed at the Haigh mill to inspect and certify each wagonload of wire before it went to the Bridge, but between mill and Bridge a switch was made. Wagon and driver pulled into a building, the approved wire was replaced with an equal quantity of rejected wire, then wagon and driver went on to the Bridge, while the good wire was returned to the mill to be run past the inspectors all over again. By the time Haigh was found out a lot of bad wire had gone into the cables, a realization that raised desperate cries from the trustees.

Roebling figured that Haigh had taken them for roughly $300,000. But the bad wire could stay in the cables, he announced. In his original calculations he had included the possibility of some such problem arising and had made the cables more than strong enough to compensate. Yet the thought that such corruption was literally woven into the Bridge could never be forgotten, least of all by Roebling himself.

As a consequence of "The Great Wire Fraud," the Roebling company, from which he had severed connections, was awarded the contract, as it should have been in the first place. That Roebling wire was the finest on the market and fairly priced had never been disputed. But Hewitt, who held the mortgage on Haigh's mill, had convinced the board that use of Roebling wire on a Roebling bridge represented a gross conflict of interest.

In the large scrapbook she kept of the newspaper coverage given all things pertaining to the Bridge and her husband, Emily Roebling later inserted a small item reporting that J. Lloyd Haigh was breaking rocks at Sing Sing.

She was her husband's representative at such lavish, publicized affairs as the 1880 dinner at Delmonico's for Ferdinand de Lesseps, the hero of the Suez Canal, which had opened the year work on the Bridge was begun. She was her husband's staunch defender when, in the very last part of the work, some newly appointed trustees led by Seth Low tried to fire Roebling from his job—in a "spirit of reform"—and almost succeeded. Finally, it was she, at his request, who was first to ride over the Bridge by carriage, in advance of the official opening. She went in an open Victoria, carrying a rooster as a symbol of victory.

The grand opening took place on May 24, 1883, and was cause for the biggest celebration ever seen in Brooklyn or New York. The President of the United States, Chester A. Arthur, a New Yorker, led the parade over the Bridge to Brooklyn, accompanied by a future President, Governor Grover Cleveland. The work had taken nearly three times as long as the five years John A. Roebling had estimated, and the cost had come to nearly $16 million, or more than twice his original figure.

The cost must also include the life of John A. Roebling and the others who followed. John French, a rigger, John McGarrity, a laborer, and Thomas

Douglass, a stonemason, were killed when a derrick fell. Henry Supple, another rigger and "one of the best men upon the Bridge," had the top of his head taken off when a strand of wire snapped. Thomas Blake was killed in the same accident. Ross Harris died in a fall. August Denning died in a fall. Hensen, Read, Delaney, Collins, Noone, McCann, Elliot, Higgens, and two men named Murphy died in falls. McLaughlin, a machinist, was "killed instantly" by a falling stone. Dougherty was crushed to death by a falling derrick. So was Enright. Mullin was crushed by a stone being swung into place. Cope, a rigger, had the job of guiding a wire rope onto a hoisting drum. When he saw the rope was not running as it should, he kicked at it. His foot slipped and his leg was wound around the drum, crushing it so

President Chester A. Arthur during his ceremonial march across the Bridge from New York to Brooklyn. *Harper's Weekly.*

138

badly he died "almost instantly." Brown lingered on in the hospital before he died. His back had been broken when a coal bucket fell on him.

Those known to have died of the bends include John Myer, Patrick McKay, and an Englishman named Reardon, who began work on the New York caisson on May 17, 1872, and died May 18, the day Roebling ordered the halt.

According to an interview in the *Eagle* with C. C. Martin of Roebling's staff, two others named Deneiss and Gardiner also died—though Martin could not recall how—which brings the rough total to twenty-seven.

The grief and hardship experienced are of course immeasurable. In an official report of the trustees, as an example, it is recorded that the widow of Henry Supple received as compensation for her loss $250. Because the family of John McGarran, who was permanently disabled by a fall, found themselves "entirely destitute," he was awarded $100. To what degree other victims of the bends suffered as Roebling did, or died an early death because of the ordeal, we can only imagine.

Roebling himself, incredibly, outlasted all the others on his staff. Emily, who later earned a law degree and became known for her efforts in behalf of women's suffrage, died in 1903. He was the last leaf on the tree, as he said, absorbed in his books, his greenhouse, his minerals, the wire business, feuds with his brothers, and in writing long letters to his adored son. The few times he is known to have gone out on the Bridge, with Emily and later by himself, he did so with no fanfare. Confusion over whether he or his father built the Bridge dogged him until the end. "Most people think I died in 1869," he wrote.

He died in Trenton in his own bed at age eighty-nine on July 21, 1926, almost fifty-seven years to the day after his father's death in Brooklyn.

Interestingly, those who worked on the Bridge had little or nothing to say about it once it was finished. All the speeches and poetry, the long essays, the editorials extolling its beauty and significance were provided by others. Roebling, too, said almost nothing on the subject. He, they all, seemed to prefer to let their work speak for itself.

Crossing the River: The Alternatives

Barbara Head Millstein

T‍he most important fact about the East River is that it is not a river at all.

As early as 1679-80, two ministers of a secretive religious sect called Labadists, Jasper Dankers and Peter Sluyter, recorded in their journal that "the water by which it [Long Island] is separated from 'Mahatans' is improperly called the East River, for it is nothing else than an arm of the sea beginning in the bay on the West and ending in the sea on the East." Between lecturing the native Indians and Dutch settlers on their morals, the two holy men were careful observers of the geography and customs they encountered. "There is a ferry for the purpose of crossing over it," they wrote, "which is farmed out by the year and yields a good income, as it is a considerable thoroughfare, this island [Manhattan] being one of the most populous places in the vicinity. . . . The fare over the ferry is three stuivers in zeewan for each person." Zeewan was Indian shell money, and three stuivers amounted to less than half a cent when the Dankers and Sluyter journal was first published in 1867.[1]

The ferry these two travelers used was no more than a rowboat, which in good weather carried a sail and accommodated two passengers and the ferryman. Such tiny ferries had been running for about forty years between what is now Peck Slip in Manhattan and what is now Fulton Street in Brooklyn, the first having been established sometime between 1638 and 1642. The earliest recorded ferryman was Cornelius Dircksen, who "had a farm of sixteen acres on the Brooklyn side, near the ferry, and came at the call of a horn which hung against a tree, and ferried passengers across the river in a skiff." He charged exactly the same fare as Dankers and Sluyter were to experience forty or more years later.[2]

With its landings sited at the East River's narrowest point, the ferry was the only means of passage between Manhattan, Brooklyn, and Long Island, and crossing this stretch of water, whether river or non-river, was critically important to the rural Long Island communities that sold their produce in the city.

In July 1654, "in consequence of the daily confusion occurring among ferrymen on Manhattan Island so that the inhabitants are waiting whole days before they can obtain passage and then not without danger and at an exorbitant price,"[3] the Director of the Common Council of New Amsterdam found it necessary to enact an ordinance to license ferrymen, to ensure that lodges be set up for the benefit of passengers on both sides of the river, and to establish appropriate tolls for people and for animals. Nevertheless, although it brought about legal enactments to regulate the ferries, under Dutch control the City of New Amsterdam never held a ferry as a municipal possession. By 1686, however, during the period of English rule, the inhabitants of Brooklyn, particularly the freeholders—perhaps fearful of encroachment by New York—had applied to Governor Thomas Dongan for the legal rights to operate their ferries. Here was the first indication that conflicting interests would cause ferry rights to be a subject of contention until the incorporation of the boroughs into New York City in 1898.

By all accounts, with occasional exceptions (including alternatives such as that of Hezekiah B. Pierrepont, a wealthy eccentric who used his own rowboat to make the trip daily between Brooklyn Heights and Wall Street), the ferries remained the only direct means of passenger travel between Manhattan, Brooklyn, and Long Island until the opening of the suspension bridge over the East River in 1883.

The ferries—subject to wind, weather, and tide—were a constant source of irritation to regular travelers, especially before the nineteenth century. Prior to the year 1814, "the only boats used on the East River were row boats, flat scows, or two-masted sail boats."[4] At slack water, or with a moderate current, it was a safe, comfortable trip. But against an angry flood or rapid ebb, the boatmen could make little or no headway. Often a brisk wind would blow the little boats toward Governors Island; a gale or even a stiff breeze could upend a scow-load of cattle. And so by 1800, letters suggesting alternate methods of crossing the river began to appear in newspapers as far away as Albany.

General Jeremiah Johnson, a hero of the Revolutionary War and resident of Brooklyn, made what is perhaps the first published comment in "A Topographical View of the Township of Brooklyn in Kings County, State of New York," a pamphlet printed in Brooklyn in 1800 by Thomas Kirk. Johnson wrote: "It has been suggested that a bridge should be constructed across the East River to New York. This idea has been treated as chimerical from the magnitude of the design, but whosoever takes it into their serious consideration will find more weight in the practicability of the scheme than at first sight he imagines . . . A plan has already been laid down on paper, and a gentleman of acknowledged abilities and good sense has observed that he would engage to erect it in two years time."[5] The gentleman Johnson referred

The first Brooklyn ferry master

141

to was probably Thomas Pope, who would eleven years later publish details of his "Flying Pendent Lever Bridge."

In 1802, the inhabitants of New York City and Long Island petitioned the New York State Legislature stating that "the insular situation of Long Island and the City of New York renders an intercourse between them at all times uncertain and sometimes impracticable as the only communication is by means of a ferry near a mile in length across an impetuous tide. The great and increasing population of the City of New York renders a daily supply from the country of the necessaries of life almost indispensable. It has therefore become an object of great importance . . . that a bridge should be established between them."[5]

Although the Legislature apparently did not respond, the petition excited much comment in the press, and the very next day, February 19, 1802, two letters appeared in local newspapers. In the New York *Daily Advertiser*, a correspondent calling himself "Hydraulicus" approached the matter from the basis of national security, pointing out that a bridge would enable American forces to retaliate more easily should an enemy of the United States land a small number of troops on Long Island and try to command New York City from the militarily important Brooklyn Heights. His reply also expressed concern that a bridge "must not impede or injure navigation," and he put forward the alternative idea of a dam extending from one island to the other, which would destroy the variable and dangerous current "in the arm of the sea [the East River] . . . . For communication between the [Long Island] Sound and the North River [the Hudson River], it would be necessary only to construct a lock in the dam . . . . This lock should be placed on the New York side. . . . The dam should be constructed of sufficient breadth for a handsome road to be made on its top." However, that same day the New York *Mercantile Advertiser* included a letter signed "Common Sense" warning that a bridge built on piers would alter the river's current "so that nothing but small rowboats could pass safely except at slack tide." This letter supported the status quo, whereby "intercourse between New York and Brooklyn is carried on by means of twelve boats and 24 men. . . . The men are paid 10 dollars per month. . . . The whole expense is about 20 dollars per day or $600 per month. It is supposed to be the cheapest ferry in the world."[6]

Other comments in other publications followed. One "New Yorker" predicted that "several foundations sunk in the river for a bridge to rest upon" would cause ice floes in winter to mount up. "It is seriously apprehended," he wrote, "that the obstruction occasioned by a Bridge will materially injure the harbor." Another amused but irritated reader calling himself "Caligula" posed the question: "Would it not be a greater convenience to the public . . . to erect a bridge from the Battery [in New York] to Elizabeth town [Elizabeth, New Jersey]," or even from Boston to Philadelphia. Such a bridge, he joked, would be a "pleasant crossing for the strawberries."[7]

And so the arguments continued. On February 28, 1807, John Stevens—scientist, inventor, and founder of the Stevens Institute for engineering in Hoboken, New Jersey—presented a petition to the United States Congress in which he stated that he had invented "a plan for floating bridges over waters." The matter being in his opinion "one of the national interest," he suggested the formation of a company under federal supervision "to be known as 'The United States Bridge Company.'"[8] The concept called for "Hollow vessels, well hooped with copper, 42 feet in length, 3 feet and a half in the middle, and 20 inches at each end enclosed in framework with string pieces fastened to the frames by chains, . . . with plank to be laid on top . . . and a railing on each side." Thus the petition continued in ever-growing detail, concluding with the recommendation that, where needed for navigation, parts of the bridge would operate as hinged drawbridges, being

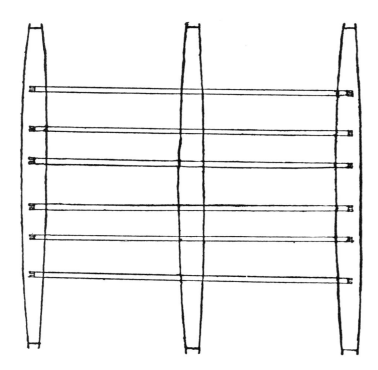

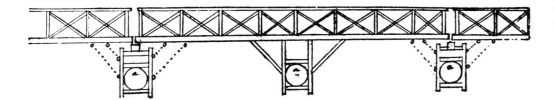

The floating bridge drawn by
Colonel John Stevens

anchored to blocks sunk at the riverside, and being raised and lowered by means of cables "so that they may fly open and shut in an instant."

The estimated cost of the bridge was ridiculously low, even for that time. It came to $40,000 (or $24,375 without the drawbridges). Stevens considered his floating bridge well suited to either the Hudson River or the East River, where he believed weather conditions would permit its use for at least eight months of the year. He sought a seven-to-ten year charter. The clamor sent up by the public against the floating bridge was great and immediate. Small vessels crisscrossed the rivers carrying signs reading: "Floating Bridges? Never while we are alive to fight them!" Congress heard the message, and the charter failed.[9]

Undaunted, the Colonel promptly came up with a second plan—one which he most probably had in mind all along, and which explained his interest in seeking a long charter. He now proposed "a permanent bridge with reaches of so great a height and so wide a span as to admit vessels of every description to pass freely. . . . In a military point of view, the advantages of bridges cannot be overlooked; . . . [those] now proposed would not only intercept the passage of enemy ships of war, but they would afford direct communication so that succor and supplies could at all times be thrown into the city."[10] This suggestion was also ignored, but not before Stevens had obtained legislative authority to present a detailed bill on the organization of the bridge company and had published this second plan in at least three newspapers. Stevens even suggested ways of paying for the bridges: one was to bring New Jersey drinking water into New York City by way of an aqueduct; another was to erect houses on the bridges as the English had done in London.

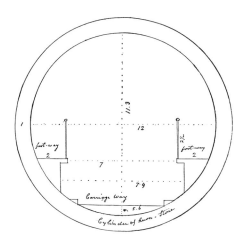

The Stevens tunnel drawn in cross-section by its inventor

The David Bates Douglas tunnel proposed for the East River
Collection: The Long Island Historical Society, New York

Having failed with bridges, Stevens—still unshaken—now proposed a tunnel, or tunnels, again for use with either river. This third plan called for the building of "cylinders of timber, each in the form of the frustrum of a cone [a section between the top and the bottom of a cone]." As many of these cylinders as the width of the river dictated would be driven together, surrounded with frames, lined with brick or hewn stone, and sunk in the silt of the riverbed. When the structure had settled, the water would be pumped out and a roadway would be constructed through the tunnel. The initial proposal called for a tunnel eight feet in diameter that would permit the passage of carriages without tops. If the prototype proved successful, two fourteen-foot-diameter tunnels would follow. The interruption to river traffic inherent in the construction system was considered negligible in view of the ultimate benefits.[11]

Although it met with the same lack of success as his previous ideas for crossing the river, this last proposal by Colonel Stevens may have influenced Major David Bates Douglas. A graduate of West Point, designer of Green-wood Cemetery in Brooklyn, and Chief Engineer of the Morris Canal in New Jersey, Bates Douglas put forward a tunnel concept, probably in the early 1830s, that also involved a structure to be laid on the bed of the river. He chose as the site for his projected tunnel the point in the East River at which the Brooklyn Bridge would eventually be built.

In 1811, a treatise entitled "A Mathematical Description of the Flying Pendent Lever Bridge" was published by Thomas Pope. Pope, who described himself as both an architect and a landscape gardener, so called his bridge because its arms were to "spring from the abutment on each side and extend

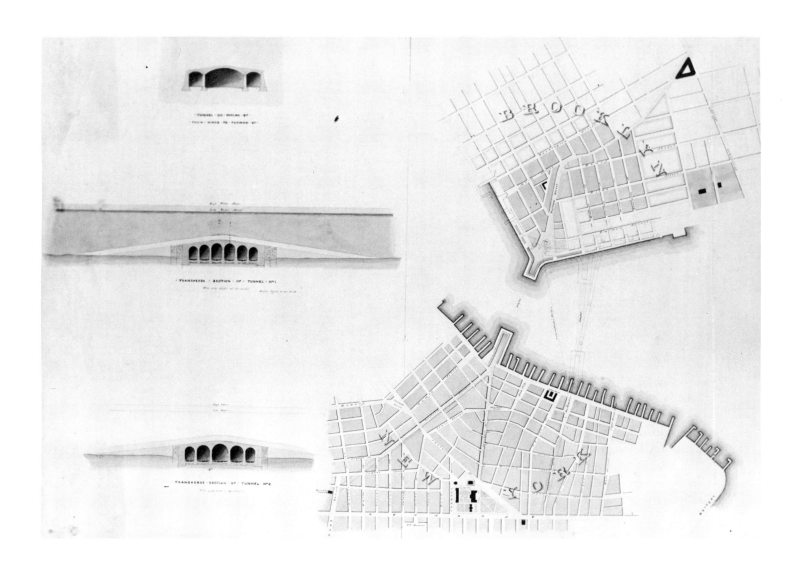

Thomas Pope's Flying Pendent Lever Bridge, also called the "Rainbow Bridge," and some of the detail drawings of its proposed construction
Courtesy: Engineering Society Library, New York

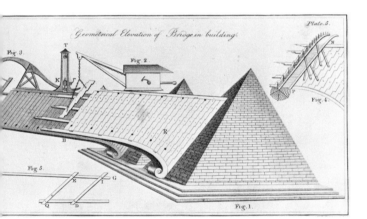

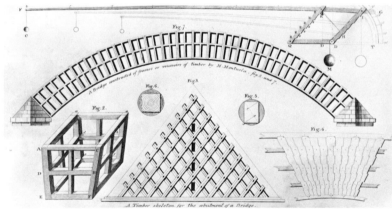

over the river ... till they meet in the center and form one single arc." The conclusion of his treatise was in the form of a lengthy poem in which he also likened his bridge to a rainbow:

> ... That half an arc should stand upon the ground,
>   Without support while building, or a rest;
>   This caus'd the theorist's rage and sceptic's jest.
>   Like half a rainbow rising on one shore,
>   While its twin partner spans the semi o'er,
>   And makes a perfect whole, that need not part,
>   Till time has furnish'd us a nobler art ... [12]

Pope proposed that his "Rainbow Bridge" be constructed of trussed logs so that repairs or replacements could be made by the simple expedient of using a common wooden ladder set up against the bridge on either side. But his theory omitted any idea of how to deal with the problems of maintenance in the middle of the bridge. To further his cause, Pope actually completed a model of his bridge in a field behind his house on Manhattan's Canal Street. On the very day that his critics came to review the structure, however, it was destroyed by lightning.

With the advent of steam power, crossing the river by ferry boat became a safer, more comfortable, and more reliable ride. The *Long Island Star* of Monday, May 11, 1814, reported: "On Sunday last commenced running the new and beautiful steamboat *Nassau* as a ferry boat between New York and Brooklyn."[13] Regular and efficient ferry service continued into the present century, but the steady stream of suggestions for alternate means of travel across the river continued unabated, and, by the 1850s, a new scheme or a new idea was appearing almost every month.

In 1855, Colonel Julius W. Adams, a Brooklynite and civil engineer, began to discuss his idea for a suspension bridge, and by 1865 he had succeeded in maturing a plan which he believed to be practicable. He proposed that the bridge be built from Fulton Ferry in Brooklyn to a point near Chatham Square on the New York side, with the main body constructed of two tubes, elliptical in section, placed side by side and supported by ribbons of steel. Travelers would cross by way of three platforms laid through the tubes.[14] As a direct result of Adams' suggestion a law chartering a bridge company was passed by the United States Congress on April 16, 1865. It was only because of his inexperience that Adams was later passed over as a bridge builder in favor of John Roebling.

The most far-reaching of all the plans for spanning the East River was published in the Brooklyn *Eagle* on January 28, 1867. Called the "Brooklyn Combination Bridge," it would, according to the article, "have four terminations starting from points widely separated, converging to one common center—in other words, two bridges built at an angle intersect each other, strengthening each other against horizontal forces and possessing all the advantages to the travelling public of two separate bridges." It would carry horsecars and carriages and, in separate lanes, pedestrians. The starting points for the X-shaped bridge would be Fulton Street and Brooklyn Heights in Brooklyn, and Burling Slip and Peck Slip in Manhattan.[15]

The least known and most complex idea was put forth by a civil engineer named Alfred P. Boller. It was presented to, and published by, the American Institute of the City of New York in 1866. The Institute was founded in 1865 to present new ideas in science with an emphasis on engineering, and its founder-members included William Vanderbilt, Alexander T. Stewart, Ezra Corning, John Jacob Astor, and A. A. Low.

Mr. Boller's bridge would have crossed from Rutgers Street in Brooklyn to Chatham Square in Manhattan. It was to be built of either "tubular girders, a trussed girder, a suspension bridge or the suspension trussed girder." Boller mentioned in his report that he would "leave out the arch system altogether since its want of adaptability to the crossing of the East River strikes even a professional man at once." The cost was estimated at $750,000. The plan called for the bridge to be built over the river on pontoons, and then raised into position by hydraulic presses. This was certainly the most sophisticated plan ever presented.[16]

The terrible winter of 1867 was probably the turning point that finally forced the issue of a bridge. According to Henry R. Stiles, on January 23, 1867, "the East River between Brooklyn and New York was bridged over by ice." By the dawn of that morning, a trio of men left Beekman Street in Manhattan and walked across the river to the Brooklyn shore, ending up at what was then "DeForrest's Stores, a couple of blocks below the city flour mills." Soon almost five thousand people had crossed the river "on foot and for nothing." As the ice began to break up, ships were damaged and about thirty people drifted to Governors Island on an ice floe. The ferry service ceased for several days.[17]

The successful bridge engineer John Roebling and his son Washington had experienced a severe winter earlier in 1852, when it took several hours to cross the river because of ice floes. (The river also froze in 1856.) Neither John nor Washington ever forgot that trip, and it was partly with this memory in mind that John Roebling presented his plan for a suspension bridge. In the time between 1856, when Roebling drew up his first rough plans, and 1864, when he published them for the third time, the Civil War had been fought. With the coming of peace, public concern turned to other matters, and, in 1865, the Bridge Company was formed. The company was chartered in 1867—the year of the big freeze—and Roebling was made chief engineer. It was clearly the right time and the right place for the right man. The Great East River Bridge was begun.

1 Jasper Dankers and Peter Sluyter, *Journal of a Voyage to New York* (Ann Arbor: University Microfilms, 1966), pp. 119-120.
2 Bibliography ref. 24, p. 444.
3 Bibliography ref. 24, p. 425.
4 Bibliography ref. 24, p. 431.
5 Bibliography ref. 24, p. 103.
6 Bibliography ref. 25, vol. 5, p. 1389.
7 Bibliography ref. 25, vol. 5, p . 1390.
8 Bibliography ref. 25, vol. 5, p. 1454.
9 Bibliography ref. 27, pp. 217-219.
10 Bibliography ref. 27, p. 220.
11 Bibliography ref. 27, p. 222.
12 Thomas Pope, *Treatise on Bridge Architecture in which the Superior Advantages of the Flying Pendent Lever Bridge are Fully Proved* (New York: Alexander Niven, 1811), p. 203 and p. 281.
13 Bibliography ref. 24, p. 434.
14 Bibliography ref. 24, p. 447.
15 The Brooklyn *Eagle* (January 28, 1867); clipping in the files of The Long Island Historical Society.
16 *Annual Report of The American Institute of the City of New York for the years 1866 & 1867* (Albany: Charles Van Benthuysen and Sons), p. 894.
17 Henry R. Stiles, *A History of Brooklyn including the Old Town and the Village of Brooklyn, the Town of Bushwick and the Village of Williamsburgh* (Brooklyn: Published by subscription, 1869-1870), vol. 2, p. 488.

Urban Design: The Bridge and Prospect Park

Albert Fein

The end of the Civil War heralded an era of optimism in which designers sought to plan the New York metropolitan area utilizing advanced technology to meet social needs with aesthetic distinction. Within this historic context two of this nation's most notable urban artifacts were built—the Brooklyn Bridge and the city of Brooklyn's park system—representing parallel efforts to create physical forms to satisfy urban needs. John Augustus Roebling and his eldest son, Washington A., were the designers and the chief engineers of the Bridge (see illustrations, pages 12 and 13), and Frederick Law Olmsted and Calvert Vaux were the landscape architects of Prospect Park and Brooklyn's innovative parkways. Sharing similar ideals, these men were able, in the details of their plans, to express the highest aspirations of their age, including a commitment to an aesthetic of functionalism. Successful completion of such large public undertakings required the political support of James S.T. Stranahan, a wealthy and influential Brooklyn businessman, as well as a system of management involving the cooperation of others. A major contributor to the building of the Bridge and the Park was Charles Cyril Martin, a civil engineer who served as "executive officer" on the construction of both projects.[1]

Both designs were part of an idealistic plan for expanding the independent cities of Brooklyn and New York into America's principal metropolis. The Bridge was needed to facilitate travel of forty million people annually across the East River—mostly Brooklyn's working-class population, which included many immigrants. Prospect Park, on the other hand, was deemed essential for "recuperation" from work—recreation—as well as for attracting visitors from New York and elsewhere. The aim was to provide Brooklyn with a public space at least equal to New York's Central Park, also designed by Olmsted and Vaux. These projects were seen as spurs to Brooklyn's development, as most of its land was still vacant; they would also increase real estate values and attract a larger middle class. The two cities would become more equal—economically, socially, and physically—with a bridge, parks, and parkways linking them into an organic whole.[2]

With the war over, the North could confront its urban ills. The Bridge and the Park symbolized a democracy's faith in its capacity to solve serious problems. The designers of these related undertakings had been strong supporters of the war and its social ideals. John Roebling and Frederick Olmsted had been ardent opponents of the institution of slavery; Washington Roebling had served valiantly as a volunteer, at least once on the same battlefield—Gettysburg—where Olmsted, as Executive Secretary of the United States Sanitary Commission, supervised the care of the wounded and the evacuation of the dead. The spirit of the times emerged most clearly in the written plans for the Bridge and the Park, both completed within two years of the fall of the Confederacy.[3]

The designers shared other sources of influence: ideas of various utopian theorists, model communities, and an urban planning tradition brought by Europeans. Inherent in utopian thought was a commitment to social change through physical planning. Significantly, the communities admired were small in scale and exhibited careful attention to basic details of civic design. Many of these settlements were founded by German immigrants adapting a planning and design experience that could be nurtured in cities like New York and Brooklyn, which had large and growing German populations.[4]

John Roebling, born and educated in Germany, and Frederick Olmsted, a Connecticut Yankee, were influenced by these antecedents, which balanced careful attention to the social quality of life with a regard for technology and scale. Saxonburg, the agricultural community Roebling founded in Pennsylvania, probably emulated the very successful utopian community of the United Society of Germans in nearby Harmony, Pennsylvania. As Washington Roebling recalled, the planning of Saxonburg streets and homes "was done in true German style."[5] Olmsted wrote admiringly of the "ideal" free-labor communities established by German utopian settlers in West Texas, which he visited in the 1850s. For him as well as for Roebling, physical form was an *international* expression of social and design influence.[6]

The most complete statement of aesthetic thought summarizing this meaning of design was penned by Leopold Eidlitz, a Prague-born American architect who appreciated the significance of the Bridge and the Park as public architecture. In his book *The Nature and Function of Art, More Especially of Architecture* (1881), Eidlitz explained the importance of functionalism to a post-Civil War generation. He believed that the medieval period provided the fullest range of building types adaptable to the needs of the time.[7]

Ideas, however, could not have been effective without political leadership. Fortunately, the growing metropolis had such notable citizens as James S.T. Stranahan, who understood Brooklyn to be part of a region requiring large-scale planning. He led the movement for a nationally innovative park system while contributing to the completion of the Bridge, serving as President of the Brooklyn Park Commission (1860-1882) and as a trustee of the Bridge (1869-1885). His final years were devoted to the political unification of the city of New York.[8]

Few could appreciate the interconnection between the Bridge, the Park, and Brooklyn's social and economic development as well as Stranahan, who was responsible for the design of the Atlantic Dock Company's waterfront property and manager of the Union Ferry Company, which operated all five lines connecting Brooklyn with New York. He understood that notwithstanding growth in population and industry Brooklyn could not compete commercially with New York. It was also losing its attraction as a residential area; an East River bridge and open space were needed to draw homeowners.[9] Stranahan fostered high levels of performance from the designers. Hoping to make Brooklyn an effective link within a national transportation system, he sought to have the Bridge reinforced to bear the weight of Pullman cars and freight trains; he encouraged the builders of the Park to plan for more diverse uses.[10]

Such a supportive atmosphere helps us to understand why these projects reflected similar ideals—construction, function, form—and collaboration in design. The technological achievement of the Bridge, the dramatic use of steel, was uniformly acclaimed. The noted architectural critic Montgomery Schuyler,

Village of Saxonburg "drawn from nature" by T. Gosewisch in July 1835. From a lithograph printed by a member of the Roebling family in Mülhausen, Germany.
Collection: Mr. and Mrs. Paul Roebling, New York

Frederick Law Olmsted
American, 1822-1903
and **Calvert Vaux**
American, 1824-1895
Design for Prospect Park 1866-67
Collection: Dumbarton Oaks,
Washington, D.C.

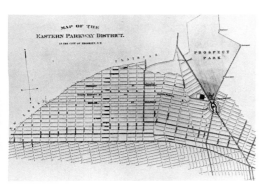

Frederick Law Olmsted
and **Calvert Vaux**
Map of the Eastern Parkway
District of Brooklyn including
Prospect Park
Collection: The Long Island Historical
Society, New York

Stores and warehouses under the
New York approach to the
Brooklyn Bridge *circa* 1905
Collection: Municipal Archives of the
City of New York

who had reservations about the form of the Bridge's towers, nonetheless declared it "one of the mechanical wonders of the world." An admirer of Olmsted, Schuyler probably also recognized the Park's modernity of construction; there was constant experimentation with materials and machinery to improve park drives.[11]

Both projects incorporated meticulous study of environmental factors such as soil composition, movement of water, and topography. Washington Roebling understood, as had his father, that the success of the Bridge would depend on the location of the caissons supporting the towers (see illustrations, pages 30-31) and that these had to conform to a topographical analysis of the riverbed. Similarly, Prospect Park's topography guided the designers in devising a drainage and water system, and in utilizing geological features to create functional and attractive spaces for recreation.[12]

The well-being of the pedestrian was another shared objective. The Bridge walkway, separate and above the roads for trains and carriages, was a safe area for crossing the river and viewing the city. In organizing the Bridge to accommodate three separated systems of transportation (see illustration, page 173) the Roeblings were adapting one of Olmsted and Vaux's most influential urban design features, first introduced in Central Park and applied in Prospect Park. In addition, these public walks contained amenities conspicuously absent from most city streets. The Bridge's elevated promenade, planned as a modern street, had benches, lighting, and even ice water in summer. The Park, almost from the day construction commenced, had seats, drinking water, and toilets.[13]

Planners of both projects were aware that success would be affected by the conditions at the entrances to their work. Adequate space was needed to accommodate thousands of anticipated users. The Bridge's Manhattan terminus was placed opposite City Hall Park. In Brooklyn a handsome public square was planned but never built. Olmsted and Vaux constructed Brooklyn's only "plaza," a large oval space serving as an entranceway to the Park and as a site for civic celebrations such as the one that took place on the opening day of the Bridge.[14]

Urban design also included concern for the kinds of land use that would occur at the edges of these projects. In stark contrast to many of the bridges and highways of the twentieth century, Brooklyn's Bridge, Park, and parkways were planned as urban complexes, not as isolated structures. Stores and a marketplace (see illustration below) were proposed as component parts of the Bridge's New York approach. These amenities were fronted by a street facilitating access to the Bridge and improving the view from below. Since Prospect Park was planned as the center of new communities, the contiguous land was integral to the design. As the Park was deemed unsafe after dark, wide sidewalks—promenades—were constructed for nighttime use. Walks and seating were also planned within the nation's first parkways—Eastern and Ocean—patterned after the boulevards of Paris. Designed as linear parks and as a new type of avenue, they became the spines along which neighborhoods have developed.[16]

Both projects conformed to an aesthetic of functionalism best captured in Leopold Eidlitz's treatise on architecture. There is, however, a major difference in the application of functionalism to land design which sets it off from that which relates to architecture and engineering. In landscape architecture the form of the land guides planning more so than in architecture or engineering.

As a result, there are obvious differences between the towers of the Bridge and the arches in the Park. The height of the towers was dictated by engineering requirements, their form by a desire to create monumental entranceways into a metropolis. Prospect Park's first arches—Endale and Meadowport—were built to separate traffic and were designed to be low and partially hidden by overhanging shrubs, blending into the landscape even as they served as passageways into Brooklyn's largest public common—the Long Meadow. Other features of the Park's architecture, designed by Vaux in stone and wood, embody a concern with romantic and picturesque details that would be irrelevant in the Bridge.

The similarities, however, also are apparent. The towers of the Bridge and the arches over the pathways of the Park were meant to appear solid and permanent, symbolizing the strength of the democratic society that produced them. American designers were sensitive to the criticism often made by European visitors that their heterogeneous, changeable nation was incapable of such achievements; further, some of the European intellectuals most respected in this country, such as the English aesthetician John Ruskin, had been extremely critical of the Civil War, viewing it as a failure of the democratic system. Yet, Ruskin's design influence, like that of the American sculptor Horatio Greenough, was reflected in the choice of materials. Democratic ornament was to be shaped out of indigenous stone, carved to emphasize its lithic and tonal qualities. The towers soaring skyward and the arches framing the ground below symbolized a deep-rooted Transcendentalist ideal: to live harmoniously with Nature's elements.[16]

The designers of the Bridge and the Park knew that their work would be subject to public review. Washington Roebling invited a committee of three prominent architects—Joseph M. Wilson, George B. Post, and Napoleon LeBrun—to examine the design of the Bridge, giving special attention to the towers; their general approval was quickly forthcoming. Olmsted and Vaux saw no need for such a formal critique. Nevertheless, like Roebling, they did seek appreciation of their work as art. In 1866 a handsomely-colored map of the Park was part of a major art show at the Brooklyn Academy of Music, and in 1876 a huge drawing of the Bridge was exhibited at the Philadelphia Centennial.[17]

There were less visible similarities basic to the construction of the Bridge and the Park. Both projects issued from much careful pre-construction study, a general plan, and a very disciplined system of work in which the chief designers were concerned with every aspect of construction. This system, while clearly hierarchical, depended to a great extent on a collaborative process of adaptation and invention as a means of solving unique problems. The Roeblings' work relationship had been such that after the father's death, the son could fully carry out the plans as conceived. A creative partnership existed between Olmsted and Vaux, who during the period they were working on Prospect Park established a new profession of landscape architecture, reflected in their designs for park systems in Buffalo and Chicago.

While it is customary to attribute the success of such complex projects to the chief designers, the reality is that all such undertakings rely on a system that utilizes diverse talents and skills, and, of course, labor. In this regard, the efforts of Charles Cyril Martin, an experienced engineer, are most instructive since he contributed to both ventures. Martin supervised the initial engineering of the Park (1867-70) and moved on to become one of Washington Roebling's very able group of assistants (see illustration, page 127). He oversaw the construction of Prospect Park's most important and unique technological invention, a great well capable of supplying all of the Park's water needs. During Roebling's long illness, it was Martin who managed the daily work on the Bridge, succeeding him as Chief Engineer and Superintendent in 1883.[18]

Such a system of cooperation was not permanent. Like all other aspects of the design process, it depended on the complex interplay of individuals within the historical circumstances of a given period. By 1883, when the Bridge was completed, it was clear that the particular amalgam of factors that led to its creation no longer existed. Much of the idealism of the post-Civil War period had diminished. Stranahan's political influence was on the wane. In 1882 he was removed as President of the Park Commission and his position as a trustee of the Bridge was threatened.[19] At the same time, a new set of aesthetic postulates was beginning to gain force: a Neoclassical Renaissance style would become dominant in many aspects of urban design.

Still, the Bridge and the Park have achieved a permanency in the social and physical life of the city that even time and changing taste have not easily affected. They continue to serve millions in essential ways. In recent years, a fuller appreciation of the creativity of both projects has emerged.[20] In the context of this awareness, which is part of a new historical condition, the Bridge and the Park may again be viewed as parallel symbols of a social process in which political leadership was able to support creative design talent in response to needs as compelling a century ago as they are today.

1   Bibliography ref. 8; *Annual Reports of the Brooklyn Park Commissioners, 1861-1873* (Brooklyn, 1873); bibliography ref. 16; bibliography ref. 26; Clay Lancaster, *Prospect Park Handbook* (New York: Long Island University Press, 1972); Albert Fein, "Historical Research and Analysis," in Anthony Walmsley, *The First Historic Landscape Report for the "Ravine District," Prospect Park, Brooklyn, New York* (unpublished report, New York City Department of Parks and Recreation, 1982); bibliography ref. 19; John David Sigle, "Bibliography of the Life and Works of Calvert Vaux," in *the American Association of Architectural Bibliographers: Papers, Volume 5, 1968*, ed. William B. O'Neal (Charlottesville: University of Virginia Press, 1968), pp. 69-93; Laura W. Roper, *FLO: A Biography of Frederick Law Olmsted* (Baltimore: Johns Hopkins University Press, 1973); Elizabeth Stevenson, *Park Maker: A Life of Frederick Law Olmsted* (New York; Macmillan Publishing, 1977); Albert Fein, *Frederick Law Olmsted and the American Environmental Tradition* (New York: George Braziller, 1972); "Charles Cyril Martin," *Appleton's Cyclopedia of American Biography*, ed. James Grant Wilson and John Fiske, vol. 4 (New York, 1900), p. 229.
2   Bibliography ref. 16, pp. 25-27; bibliography ref. 8, "Report of J. A. Roebling," p. 31; Frederick Law Olmsted and Calvert Vaux, "Report of the Landscape Architects and Superintendents to the President of the Board of Commissioners of Prospect Park, Brooklyn (1868)" in Albert Fein, ed., *Landscape into Cityscape: Frederick Law Olmsted's Plans for a Greater New York City* (New York: Van Nostrand Reinhold Co., 1981), *passim*.
3   Johann August Roebling, *Diary of My Journey from Muehlhausen in Thuringia via Bremen to the United States of North America in the Year 1831*, trans. by Edward Underwood (Trenton, N.J.: Roebling Press, 1931), pp. 115-118; for Olmsted's views on slavery and his part in the Civil War, see Roper, *FLO*, pp. 84-91, 156-232; Stevenson, *Park Maker*, pp. 124-125, 195-246; Fein, *Frederick Law Olmsted*, pp. 17, 24, 48. Bibliography ref. 16, pp. 157-163; bibliography ref. 21, pp. 188-197.
4   Charles Nordhoff, *Communistic Societies of America* (New York: Harper & Bros., 1875); Dolores Hayden, *Seven American Utopias: The Architecture of Communitarian Socialism, 1790-1975* (Cambridge, MA: M.I.T. Press, 1975); Ira Rosenwaike, *Population History of New York City* (Syracuse, NY: Syracuse Univ. Press, 1972), pp. 67, 70.
5   Bibliography ref. 26, pp. 46-48; Chester Hale Sipe, *History of Butler County, Pennsylvania* (Indianapolis: Historical Publishing Company, 1927), vol I, pp. 40, 404-407, 411.
6   Albert Fein, "Fourierism in Nineteenth-Century America: A Social and Environmental Perspective," in Mathé Allain, ed., *France and North America: Utopia and Utopians* (Lafayette, LA: University of Southwest Louisiana, 1979), pp. 138-148; Frederick Law Olmsted, *A Journey through Texas: or, a Saddle-Trip on the Southwestern Frontier* (New York: Dix, Edwards & Co., 1857), pp. 142-143.
7   Biruta Erdmann, *Leopold Eiditz's Architectural Theories and American Transcendentalism*, doctoral dissertation (Ann Arbor: Univ. of Michigan, 1978).
8   Henry Isham Hazelton, *The Boroughs of Brooklyn and Queens, Counties of Nassau and Suffolk, Long Island, New York, 1909-1924* (New York: Lewis Historical Publishing Co., Inc., 1925), vol I, pp. 1-8.
9   *Annual Reports 1861-73*, p. 346.
10 Bibliography ref. 16, p. 482; Fein in Walmsley, *The First Historic Landscape Report*, pp. 16-19.
11 Bibliography ref. 21, p. 332; Roper, *FLO*, p. 368; Charles C. Martin to Olmsted and Vaux in *Annual Reports, 1861-73*, pp. 204, 287.
12 Bibliography ref. 8, "Report of J. A. Roebling," pp. 22-23; *Annual Reports, 1861-73*, p. 210.
13 Bibliography ref. 16, p. 32; *Annual Reports, 1861-73*, pp. 282-283, 289, 304, 424-425, 486; bibliography ref. 8, Charles C. Martin, "Report of the Chief Engineer and Superintendent," pp. 5, 8.
14 Bibliography ref. 8, "Report of J. A. Roebling," pp. 7-8; bibliography ref. 3, p. 14; *Annual Reports, 1861-73*, p. 280; *Twenty-third Annual Report of the Brooklyn Park Commissioners for the Year 1883* (Brooklyn, 1884), p. 35.
15 Bibliography ref. 8, "Report of J. A. Roebling," pp. 28-29; *Annual Reports, 1861-73*, p. 435; Fein, ed., *Landscape into Cityscape*, pp. 121, 159-164.
16 Sara Norton and M. A. DeWolfe Howe, eds., *Letters of Charles Eliot Norton I* (Boston: Houghton Mifflin Co., 1913), pp. 284-285; Roger B. Stein, *John Ruskin and Aesthetic Thought in America, 1840-1900* (Cambridge, MA: Harvard University Press, 1967); James T. Callow, *Kindred Spirits: Knickerbocker Writers and American Artists, 1807-1855* (Chapel Hill: University of North Carolina, 1967), pp. 212-213.
17 Washington A. Roebling to Napoleon LeBrun, 17 May 1877, and Joseph M. Wilson, George B. Post, and Napoleon LeBrun to Colonel W. A. Roebling, 27 June 1877, in bibliography ref. 8, pp. 3-7; Alfred J. Bloor Diary, The New-York Historical Society, 17, 20 March 1866; bibliography ref. 16, p. 350.
18 Fein, ed., *Landscape into Cityscape*, pp. 114-115; *Annual Reports, 1861-73*, pp. 354-355, 362-370; bibliography ref. 16, pp. 146, 224, 329.
19 Stranahan to Olmsted, 7 July 1882; John Y. Culyer to Olmsted, 29 January 1882; Stranahan to Olmsted, 16 March 1882—in Frederick Law Olmsted Papers, Manuscript Division, Library of Congress; Leland M. Roth, *A Concise History of American Architecture* (New York: Harper & Row, 1979), ch. 6.
20 I am referring to publications such as McCullough's and Trachtenberg's as well as to the current efforts to restore Prospect Park, which reflect a growing popular appreciation of the diverse ways in which history has become part of American culture.

Lewis Kachur

Childe Hassam
Brooklyn Bridge n.d.
Charcoal, heightened with
colored pencil on gray paper
13.0 × 20.0 cm. (5¼ × 7⅞ in.)
Collection:
Museum of Art, Carnegie Institute,
Pennsylvania, Andrew Carnegie Fund

154

Heralding the dawn of the Technological Age, signifying the linking of East and West, encompassing both Old World tradition and New World innovation in its combination of stone Gothic towers and steel cables, the Brooklyn Bridge has seized the imagination of a multitude of artists as the quintessential American emblem. The painter Joseph Stella put it this way: "Seen for the first time, as a weird metallic Apparition under a metallic sky, out of proportion with the winged lightness of its arch, traced for the conjunction of WORLDS . . . it impressed me as the shrine containing all the efforts of the new civilization of AMERICA."[1] In countless icons ranging from the representational to the surrealistic to the abstract, the Bridge has symbolized what the architectural critic Lewis Mumford called "both a fulfillment and a prophecy."

The elements of this dialectical symbolism are, of course, manifest in the Bridge itself. As Mumford wrote, "The stone plays against the steel: the heavy granite in compression, the spidery steel in tension. In this structure, the architecture of the past, massive and protective, meets the architecture of the future, light, aerial, open to sunlight, an architecture of voids rather than of solids."[2] Thus, on the one hand, the Bridge's masonry has suggested to some artists an analogy to the great cathedrals of Europe. (The French painter Albert Gleizes once observed, "the genius who built the Brooklyn Bridge is to be classed alongside the genius who built Notre Dame de Paris."[3]) On the other hand, the Bridge's openness and lack of ornamentation has led many to celebrate its machinelike crispness.

The wide range of imagery encouraged by the Bridge's synthesis of monumentality and ethereality can be seen at a glance in a comparison of the works of two artists who depicted the Bridge at the turn of the century. In a *circa* 1895 watercolor and tempera of the Bridge at twilight (see page 153), William Sonntag views the Bridge from the Brooklyn side as the last rays of sunset reflect on the inside of its tower's pointed arches. Although Manhattan was hardly frontier America, the grandeur of the image suggests that Sonntag saw the Bridge as the apotheosis of America's westward march.

Childe Hassam
American, 1859–1935
Brooklyn Bridge in Winter 1904
Oil on canvas
76.0 × 86.3 cm. (30 × 34 in.)
Collection:
The Telfair Academy of Arts and Sciences, Georgia

Glenn O. Coleman
American, 1884–1932
Bridge Tower 1929 or 1930
Oil on canvas
76.5 × 63.5 cm. (30⅛ × 25 in.)
Collection:
The Brooklyn Museum, New York
Gift of Charles Simon

George Benjamin Luks
American, 1867–1933
Brooklyn Bridge 1916
Oil on canvas
35.5 × 48.2 cm. (14 × 19 in.)
Collection:
Mr. and Mrs. Meyer P. Potamkin,
Pennsylvania

In contrast, in a somewhat later painting and the direct charcoal study on which it was based (see pages 154-155), the Impressionist Childe Hassam emphasizes the Bridge's aerial quality, placing it in the middle ground enshrouded by the winter atmosphere.

Because the painters of Sonntag and Hassam's generation were generally more interested in interiors and suburban landscapes, the Bridge did not become a popular motif until the advent of The Eight, the group of artists around Robert Henri whose rebel exhibition of 1908 led to the formation of the Ashcan School. As Henri's pupil Stuart Davis recalled in his autobiography, the Manhattan scene was a favorite subject of the Ashcan artists. "Enthusiasm for running around and drawing things in the raw ran high," Davis wrote. "In pursuance of this compulsion, Glenn Coleman [see Coleman's *Bridge Tower*, illustrated on page 155], Henry Glitenkamp, and myself toured extensively in the metropolitan environs. Chinatown; the Bowery; the burlesque shows; the Brooklyn Bridge..."[4]

Despite their reputation for gritty Realism, the Ashcan artists tended to treat the Bridge at an atmospheric distance. Like Hassam's painting, George Luks' small canvas of 1916 and Ernest Lawson's undated work of the same period are views over the rooftops in overcast weather. The similarity of the paintings by Hassam and Luks—both winter scenes with snow on the tenements—is striking. And yet there is a dramatic change in spatial treatment and tonality. While Hassam's Bridge is engulfed in a blue haze, Luks' Bridge plunges into moist grayness.

Although the Brooklyn Bridge was an inevitable component of the New York scenery the Ashcan artists recorded, it never held the fascination for them that it did for the generation of modern artists that arrived or returned from Europe in the second decade of this century (Lawson, for one, even preferred the High Bridge over the Harlem River). Many of the members of that new generation—including Joseph Stella, Albert Gleizes, John Marin, and Max Weber—dedicated a significant part of their oeuvres to the Bridge's soaring magnificence. Whether it was the contrast with the rustic bridges of the Old World that drew the modernists to the Brooklyn Bridge is not known, but it seems that the pictorial possibilities inherent in the structure were especially suited to the modern movement. Having absorbed the influence of Cubism and Futurism, these artists utilized dynamic fragmentation, overlapping transparencies, and compressed space to imaginatively re-create the Bridge on canvas.

For the architect-turned-artist John Marin, the Bridge became a leitmotif in a synthesis of modernist pictorial structure and the new urban architecture. Seeing it again upon his return from Europe in 1910, Marin was struck by the dignity and dynamism of the span. Over the next three years, he completed some fourteen watercolors and drawings of the Bridge, plus half a dozen related etchings,[5] surveying the Bridge in all its facets, from a rainbow-like arch spanning the entire width of the sheet (see below) to a frame for detailed impressions of buildings seen through the grid of its cables.[6] Marin also used the Bridge as a detail in later works, and it was probably the vantage point from which he painted still other cityscapes.

Ernest Lawson
American, 1873–1939
Brooklyn Bridge n.d.
Oil on canvas
38.4 × 48.3 cm. (15⅛ × 19)
Collection: Leslie Katz, New York

John Marin
American, 1870–1953
Brooklyn Bridge 1910
Watercolor and pencil on paper
35.5 × 43.1 cm. (14 × 17 in.)
Collection: San Diego Museum of Art, California

John Marin
American, 1870–1953
Brooklyn Bridge *circa* 1912
Watercolor on paper
46.9 × 39.3 cm. (18½ × 15½ in.)
Collection:
The Metropolitan Museum of Art,
New York, The Alfred Stieglitz Collection

Especially striking are Marin's renditions of the Bridge's pedestrian walkway. In one of these, the 1913 etching *Brooklyn Bridge*, his drypoint technique seems to stitch the building materials together. Emphasizing the majesty of the stone towers, this work exemplifies the revival of cathedral imagery in modern art (a theme that would be amplified by John Taylor Arms, a depicter of French cathedrals whose 1922 etching *Gates of the City* is probably the strongest expression of the Bridge-as-cathedral).[7] Many of

John Marin
Brooklyn Bridge 1913
Etching
Image: 28.0 × 21.7 cm. (11 × 8½ in.)
Collection:
The Brooklyn Museum, New York

John Taylor Arms
American, 1877–1953
The Gates of the City 1922
Etching and aquatint
Image: 22.9 × 21.9 cm. (9 × 8⅝ in.)
Collection: Associated American Artists,
New York

John Marin
Brooklyn Bridge No. 6 1913
Etching
Image: 27.6 × 22.3 cm. (10⅞ × 8¾ in.)
Collection: The Brooklyn Museum, New York

John Marin
Related to Brooklyn Bridge 1928
Oil on canvas
67.3 × 76.2 cm. (26½ × 30 in.)
Collection: Kennedy Galleries, Inc., New York

Max Weber
American, 1881–1961
Brooklyn Bridge 1912
Watercolor, chalk, and
charcoal on paper
48.3 × 62.2 cm. (19 × 24½ in.)
Collection:
Lionel Kelly, Reading, England

Max Weber
Brooklyn Bridge 1928
Lithograph
Image: 15.7 × 21.8 cm.
(6³⁄₁₆ × 8⁹⁄₁₆ in.)
Collection:
The Museum of Modern Art, New York
Gift of Abby Aldrich Rockefeller

Marin's other promenade scenes are less architectonic in composition, capturing instead a feeling of motion, wind, and light. In a second print from his 1913 series (*Brooklyn Bridge No. 6*) and in the watercolor of about 1912 on which the print was based (also called *Brooklyn Bridge*), the exhilaration of these sensations is so dizzying as to destabilize the structure. In the watercolor Marin adds bright splotches of red and blue to convey the impressions experienced by the strolling figures. A similar sort of energy is seen in his 1928 oil painting *Related to Brooklyn Bridge*, a night scene with blue stars dotting a luminescent sky. There the pedestrians are dwarfed by green skyscrapers and slashing brown cables, and technology appears to engulf humanity.

Marin's involvement with the Bridge was similar to that experienced by Max Weber, a fellow member of the circle of artists who gathered around the avant-garde photographer and pioneer dealer of modern art Alfred Stieglitz. Like Marin, Weber was first attracted to the Bridge when he returned to New York after a sojourn in Europe. His first views were also relatively conventional, as in a 1911 painting of the Bridge seen over rooftops (not illustrated here).[8] Then, in 1912, he painted a modernist *Brooklyn Bridge* watercolor with fluid, dynamic brushstrokes. Although this work is comparable to Marin's contemporary watercolor of the promenade, it has a greater solidity, making it an important forerunner of Joseph Stella's massive Bridge paintings. Weber gave this image to a friend, the English photographer Alvin Langdon Coburn, in 1914, but he later made a lithograph based on it. In both works, the focus is on a single monumental tower, with the lower part of the tower's arches filled in by the cables behind.

In the mid-teens, as Weber became more interested in figural compositions and Marin turned increasingly to pastoral landscapes, Albert Gleizes arrived from Europe and took up their intoxication with the Bridge. His first depiction (a 1915 work illustrated on page 110) was the most abstract image of the Bridge yet made, with criss-crossed cables forming a flat pattern analogous to the form of an aeolian harp. But his third version, a 1917 painting entitled *On Brooklyn Bridge*, is even more encompassing and symphonic. In it, Gleizes suggests the Bridge's towers amidst a rainbow of

Albert Gleizes
French, 1881–1953
On Brooklyn Bridge 1917
Oil on canvas
161.9 × 129.3 cm. (63¾ × 50⅞ in.)
Collection:
The Solomon R. Guggenheim Museum,
New York

Joseph Stella
American, 1877–1946
Brooklyn Bridge 1918–19
Oil on canvas
213.4 × 193.1 cm. (84 × 76 in.)
Collection:
Yale University Art Gallery, Connecticut
Gift of Collection Société Anonyme

colorful concentric circles derived from the Orphic Cubism of his countryman Robert Delaunay. Like Delaunay's Eiffel Tower paintings, this work is a highly optimistic view of technology unshadowed by World War I. In addition to supporting Gleizes' claim that the Bridge belongs in the same league as Notre Dame, it illustrates Marcel Duchamp's assessment that America's greatest works of art are its bridges and its plumbing.

After Gleizes returned to Paris, Joseph Stella adopted the Bridge motif. Born in Italy, Stella had immigrated to New York in 1896. During a year in Paris (1911-12) he came in contact with the Italian Futurists, who glorified machine technology and dynamic motion. Upon his return to New York he moved to Brooklyn and there found in the Bridge the perfect vehicle for his Futurist vision. "Many nights I stood on the bridge," he later recalled, "...shaken by the underground tumult of the trains in perpetual motion... now and then [hearing] strange moanings of appeal from tug boats.... I felt deeply moved, as if on the threshold of a new religion or in the presence of a new DIVINITY."[9]

Stella's *Brooklyn Bridge* of 1918-19 is probably the single most renowned rendition of the span. It is as steely and nocturnal as Gleizes' 1917 work is vivid and sunny. Flashes of red and green signal lights punctuate a deep blue

Joseph Stella
The Bridge 1920–22
panel #5 of the series
*The Voice of the City of
New York Interpreted*
Oil and tempera on canvas
224.1 × 137.2 cm. (88¼ × 54 in.)
*Collection:
Newark Museum, New Jersey
Felix Fuld Bequest
(See also preparatory sketch on p. 112)*

163

Above:
Stuart Davis
American, 1894–1964
The Barber Shop 1930
Oil on canvas
89.2 × 108.6 cm. (35⅛ × 42¾ in.)
Collection:
Neuberger Museum,
State University of New York,
College at Purchase
Gift of Roy R. Neuberger

Right:
Louis Lozowick
American, 1892–1973
Brooklyn Bridge 1930
Lithograph
Image: 33.0 × 20.0 (13 × 7⅞ in.)
Collection:
The Brooklyn Museum, New York
Gift of Erhart Weyhe

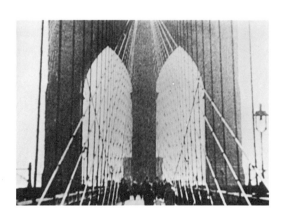

Above:
Charles Sheeler
American, 1883–1965
and **Paul Strand**
American, 1890–1976
Film still from **Mannahatta** 1921
Collection:
The Museum of Modern Art,
Film Stills Archive, New York

sky interlaced with the Bridge's flickering wire ropes. The focal point is in the upper middle, where a tripartite tower rises in front of a pair of seemingly endless crossed cables. Upon seeing this seven-foot canvas when it was first exhibited in 1920, one critic who had actually watched the Bridge being built hailed the work as "the apotheosis of the Bridge...the whole picture is throbbing, pulsating, trembling with the constant passing of the throng of cars."[10]

A more streamlined, less fragmented Bridge appears in the right-hand wing of Stella's ambitious polyptych *The Voice of the City of New York Interpreted*, painted in 1920-22. The Bridge is given equal footing with the skyscrapers, the port, and Broadway in this icon of the metropolis. Its first tower is aligned with the framing edges, reaffirming the surface while providing large, arched perforations through which the Bridge's web of wires, its second tower, and the buildings beyond are viewed. The four main cables curve in front of the first tower, implicitly in front of the picture plane, sweeping into the spectator's space. This formal innovation both engages the viewer and lends the painting its ominous, almost frightening power.

The view through the arches of one of the towers also figures in Stella's 1929 *American Landscape* (see frontispiece). By the title of that work, Stella elevates the Bridge beyond local significance to the status of national icon. He crops the first tower, through which the second tower and a skyscraper are glimpsed, at the left edge. Beyond the swing of cables to the right, the Flatiron Building is seen amidst a forest of futuristic structures which are implicitly equated with the Bridge's towers as symbols of the new America.

Many art historians have speculated that Stella's Bridge pictures, particularly *New York Interpreted*, inspired the poet Hart Crane, whose ode "To Brooklyn Bridge" (begun in the early twenties and published in 1930 with photographs by Walker Evans) may have in turn inspired such 1930s artists as Stuart Davis (see *The Barber Shop*). Crane himself seems to have felt that the similarities in their works were a product of parallel interests. In offering to help Stella get his illustrated essay on the Bridge published in the Parisian avant-garde magazine *transition* in 1929, he wrote, "It is a remarkable coincidence that I should, years later, have discovered that another person, by whom I mean you, should have had the same sentiments regarding the Brooklyn Bridge which inspired the main theme and pattern of my poem."[11]

The clarity and sleekness that Stella found in the Bridge also appealed to the so-called Precisionist movement that was popular in American visual arts of the 1920s. In film, Charles Sheeler and Paul Strand incorporated clean, architectonic images of the Bridge in their 1921 movie *Mannahatta*, which is largely a cinematic *New York Interpreted*. And in printmaking, the Ukranian immigrant Louis Lozowick included the Bridge in his streamlined 1925 lithograph *New York* (illustrated on page 111) and in one of a series of five lithographs of New York bridges that he produced in 1929-30 (illustrated on facing page).[12] Although the viewpoint in Lozowick's 1930 view (which was reproduced in the 1939 *WPA Guide to New York City*) is nearly identical to that in John Taylor Arms' *Gates of the City*, a tenser and more contemporary feeling is conveyed.

Such urban vitalism seemed inappropriate to the Magic Realists of the 1930s, who responded to the collapse of the American economy and the rise of European Fascism with surrealistic visions of doom. Thus in his 1932 mural *Wheels: Industrial New York*, Yun Gee juxtaposes the Bridge against a chaotic panorama. Born in Canton, China, Gee had arrived in New York via Paris in 1930 and had completed this work as his submission for the Museum of Modern Art's invitational mural exhibition of 1932. In the seven-by-four-foot format specified, he depicts an oversized solar disc overheating the frenzied scene and casting long, strange shadows among the polo players in the foreground. These symbolic riders circle endlessly, more like horseman of the apocalypse than sportsmen of leisure.[13]

Yun Gee
American, 1906–1963
Wheels: Industrial New York 1932
Oil on canvas
213.4 × 121.9 cm. (84 × 48 in.)
Collection:
Li–lan and Helen Gee, New York   165

Even more surrealistic interpretations of the Bridge are found among the works of O. Louis Guglielmi. Guglielmi, who had immigrated to New York with his Italian parents in 1914, first began to include symbolic images in his tightly delineated paintings in the mid-thirties. He first used the Bridge in 1935 in *South Street Stoop* (not illustrated here) and used it again the following year in a similar manner in *Wedding in South Street*. Both works are cityscapes in a minor key, reflecting the melancholy of the Depression, when the Bridge

Above:
O. Louis Guglielmi
American, 1906–1956
Wedding in South Street 1936
Oil on canvas
76.2 × 60.8 cm. (30 × 24 in.)
Collection:
The Museum of Modern Art, New York

Right:
O. Louis Guglielmi
Mental Geography 1938
Oil on canvas
90.8 × 71.1 cm. (35¾ × 24 in.)
Collection:
Barney A. Ebsworth, Missouri

seemed to stand for an earlier, better world. *Wedding*, which the artist submitted to the Federal Art Project in May 1936, struck one art historian as more funereal than celebratory.[14]

In 1938, the year after Picasso completed *Guernica*, Guglielmi painted his own antiwar masterpiece *Mental Geography*. This striking image, probably the most radical expressive distortion of the Bridge ever painted, envisages the Bridge in ruins. The seated woman in the foreground with a bomb in her

O. Louis Guglielmi
The Bridge 1942
Oil on Masonite
83.8 × 63.5 cm. (33 × 25 in.)
Collection:
Estate of Earle Ludgin, Illinois

Above:
James H. Daugherty
American, 1889–1974
Brooklyn Bridge 1944
Oil on Masonite
35.5 × 45.7 cm. (14 × 18 in.)
Collection:
Robert Schoelkopf Gallery,
New York

back signals the metaphoric intention of the image, as does the statement Guglielmi wrote when the painting was first exhibited: "Headlines, eloquent loudspeakers of Fascist destruction scream out the bombing of another city . . . Madrid, Barcelona, Guernica . . . Chartres—New York—Brooklyn Bridge is by the process of mental geography a huge mass of stone, twisted girders, and limp cable."[15] It is noteworthy that in this impassioned transmutation of the Spanish Civil War Guglielmi links the Bridge to a great French Gothic cathedral.

Following the Fascist victory in Spain, Guglielmi turned to a more personal symbolism. In his 1942 painting *The Bridge*, he views the structure as a huge musical instrument, adding a giant violin bridge to one of the Bridge's towers. This strange pun is reinforced by the semi-transparent, scroll-headed figure who grasps for the Bridge as if for a harp. Likewise, the workmen bringing a new cable can be interpreted as replacing a broken string. Guglielmi thus literalizes the metaphor of the Bridge as stringed instrument implicit in Albert Gleizes' 1915 painting and Hart Crane's verse: "fleckless the gleaming staves—/Sibylline voices flicker, waveringly stream/ As though a god were issue of the strings . . . "

Among the other artists who depicted the Bridge in the 1940s were George Grosz, James Henry Daugherty, and Georgia O'Keeffe. For the cover of Henry Miller's novel *Plexus*, published in France in 1949, Grosz, a Berlin-born satirist, painted a deep blue watercolor of the span with flocks of red birds. Daugherty, an illustrator born in North Carolina, produced an Ashcan-type genre scene in which the vivid, arching Bridge dwarfs a trio of skinnydippers. And O'Keeffe, who had painted views of the East River in the late 1920s, explored the Bridge's iconic possibilities in two works.

O'Keeffe's sketch and painting of the Bridge feature formal inventions which rival those of Joseph Stella. In both works, one of the Bridge's towers is coequal with the framing edges, and, as in Max Weber's watercolor and lithograph, the arches are tapered by the cables behind them. In the sketch, the top of the other tower is visible at the lower center, as if the front tower

George Grosz
American, 1893–1959
Brooklyn Bridge n.d.
Watercolor on paper
27.9 × 35.5 cm.
(11 × 14 in.)
Collection:
Zachary P. Morfogen,
New Jersey

Left:
Georgia O'Keeffe
Brooklyn Bridge 1949
Oil on Masonite
121.8 × 91.0 cm. (47¹⁵⁄₁₆ × 35⅞ in.)
Collection:
The Brooklyn Museum, New York
Bequest of Mary Childs Draper

Above:
Georgia O'Keeffe
American, b. 1887
Brooklyn Bridge 1949
Charcoal on brown paper
101.6 × 74.9 cm. (40 × 29½ in.)
Collection:
Doris Bry, New York   169

were transparent, or as if two views had been telescoped onto one sheet. This simultaneity imparts a complex and mysterious power to the drawing. In contrast, the painting is distant and detached, with the tower overwhelming the thin, spidery cables and flattening the pictorial space. Since these works were done just before she left New York to live in New Mexico, O'Keeffe may have intended for the Bridge to serve as a symbol of the city of her early career.

In the last thirty years, the Bridge has come to seem somewhat less modernistic (especially compared to such recent marvels as the Verrazano-Narrows Bridge and the towers of the World Trade Center), and some artists have begun to take more stylistic liberties with it. Among these artists are John Shaw, who painted an imaginative and varied series of Bridge views (not illustrated here) over an eighteen-month period from 1980 to 1981; Red Grooms, who made it the object of his humor in his zany tableau-environment *Ruckus Manhattan*; and the Greek artist Athena, who used it as a sort of giant rainbow in her huge mixed-media panorama of the crowded city. In the last two works, as in Stella's *New York Interpreted*, the Bridge is an essential feature of the artist's all-encompassing vision of the metropolis. In another vein, Richard Haas has painted a *trompe l'oeil* mural which creates an illusionary vista of the Bridge in the shadow of the real thing (see page 122).

One contemporary artist who has brought the Bridge into the age of sleek graphic design is Robert Indiana, who has lived in view of the span since he moved to a studio in lower Manhattan in 1956. Indiana's Bridge painting of 1964 (see page 120) shows a single majestic tower reproduced in four lozenge-shaped panels. The image is reduced to a logo encircled by the stenciled words of Hart Crane's poem, by now inseparable from the structure. Each panel is colored a different hue to suggest the different times of the day, as in Monet's more atmospheric series on the London bridges. The cycle begins with dawn at the right, ringed by Crane's line "silver-paced as though the sun took step of thee," and continues clockwise through day,

Red Grooms
American, b. 1937
Brooklyn Bridge 1976
from *Ruckus Manhattan*
Polychromed steel
487.8 × 365.8 × 944.4 cm.
(192 × 144 × 372 in.)
Collection: The artist
Photo: Courtesy of
Marlborough Gallery, New York

This view of the welded–metal structure of the Bridge with a careening cyclist, a freighter passing below, and a bust of John A. Roebling above was taken after the rest of *Ruckus Manhattan* had been dismantled.

sunset, and finally night at the top. Even in the year of the futuristic structures seen at the New York World's Fair, a reviewer singled out the venerable bridge of Indiana's painting as "the symbol and promise of change and the future."[16]

The majestic presence of the Brooklyn Bridge has long captured the artistic imagination without defeating it. Now, as we look forward to the second century of this "symbol and promise," it is not difficult to imagine that the growing number of artists who have recently begun living and working near the Brooklyn waterfront will discover their own meanings in the Bridge, thus creating new homages to this incomparable inspiration.

Athena
Greek, b. 1928
Brooklyn Bridge over the City 1974
Mixed media: wood, paint, and cloth
297.1 × 524.2 × 30.5 cm.
(105 × 206½ × 12 in.)
Collection:
Mr. and Mrs. Robert Ebers, New York

1   Joseph Stella, "The Brooklyn Bridge (A page of my life)," *transition* 16 (June 1929), p. 87.
2   Lewis Mumford, "The Brooklyn Bridge," *American Mercury* 23 (August 1931), p. 449.
3   Albert Gleizes quoted in *The Literary Digest* 51 (November 27, 1915), p. 1225.
4   Stuart Davis, *Stuart Davis* (New York: American Artists Group, 1945), p. 2.
5   Sheldon Reich, *John Marin* (Tucson, 1970), volume II, nos. 10.6-10.12, 11.1-11.3, 11.9, 11.21, 12.10-12.13; and Carl Zigrosser, *The Complete Etchings of John Marin* (Philadelphia, 1969), nos. 104-112.
6   The rainbow/grid duality was developed by Alan Trachtenberg, *Brooklyn Bridge: Fact and Symbol* (biblio. ref. no. 26), p. 12. The English Futurist painter C.R.W. Nevinson visited New York in 1919 and also produced an etching of a view through the cables.
7   I am indebted to Kirk Varnedoe of New York University's Institute of Fine Arts for this suggestion. See also Donat de Chapeaurouge, "Die Kathedrale als modernes Bildthema," *Jahrbuch der Hamburger Kunstsammlungen* XVIII (1973), pp. 155-172. Lyonel Feininger is another modern artist who often painted cathedrals and who made a number of drawings of the Brooklyn Bridge in the 1940s and '50s.
8   Percy North, *Max Weber: American Modern* (New York: The Jewish Museum, 1982), il. p. 56. North also discusses Weber's unpublished 1912 essay "On the Brooklyn Bridge" and concludes

that "for Weber the bridge represented a personal link between his adult life in Manhattan and his childhood in Brooklyn."
9   Stella, *Ibid*, p. 88.
10. Hamilton Easter Field, *The Arts* vol. 2, no. 1 (October 1921), p. 25.
11 Brom Weber, ed., *The Letters of Hart Crane* (New York, 1952), letter no. 317 of January 24, 1929, p. 334. For a detailed discussion of this interchange, see Irma Jaffee, "Stella and Crane," *American Art Journal* 1 (Fall 1969), pp. 98-107.
12 Janet Flint, *The Prints of Louis Lozowick: A Catalogue Raisonne* (New York, 1982), no. 6.
13 See further Judith Tannenbaum, "Yun Gee: A Rediscovery," *Arts Magazine* vol. 54, no. 9 (May 1980), p. 166, color il. p. 167.
14 Rutgers University Art Gallery, *O. Louis Guglielmi*, New Brunswick, 1980, p. 13 and fig. 27. Milton Avery also submitted a Brooklyn Bridge painting to the Federal Art Project in 1938, but it is now lost. See "An Interview with Sally Avery," *Art/World* 7, no. 1 (October 1982), p. 10. In conversation with the author, Mrs. Avery recalled that this painting was the same one awarded the Atheneum prize in 1929. To judge from an old photograph, it was an imposing, dark painting of the Bridge seen from below.
15 Rutgers, *Ibid*, pp. 20 and 23.
16 Mildred Constantine, "Visit New York Visit New York" *Art in America* 52, no. 3 (June 1964), p. 129.

The Next Hundred Years

Steven S. Ross

When talking about great projects like the Brooklyn Bridge, engineers are fond of saying that the structure itself is far greater than the sum of its parts. Unfortunately, the reverse is also true. The loss or deterioration of just a few out of the hundreds of thousands of pieces in the Brooklyn Bridge could threaten the entire structure or at least the people on it. In June 1981, for example, a pedestrian was killed while walking on the Bridge's promenade when a diagonal stay parted and whipped downward.

After almost thirty years of neglecting the Bridge, New York State has hired first-class engineering talent to make sure all those pieces are in good condition and functioning properly. To do that, the engineers have probed deep into the Bridge's structure, checking for obvious signs of deterioration and calculating the stresses borne by the various parts.

Most of the Brooklyn Bridge's users consider the structure eternal—unmoving and unchanging. To the engineers, however, the Bridge is a dynamic, living thing. In warm weather, for instance, the four main cables expand and sag a bit. At the same time, the steel beams of the truss that supports the roadway also expand, inching away from points where the truss is fixed to the main towers.

Over most of the Bridge, the vertical suspender cables and the diagonal stays adjust themselves to these shifts. But near the center of the Bridge, where the main cables dip to the level of the roadway, the truss is suspended from the main cables by very short bars. As the temperature changes, those bars can be thrust far from the vertical. They tear and break—and have done so since 1901. Now the engineers will no longer rely on periodic replacement of these bars. At the New York-based consulting firm of Steinman Boynton Gronquist & Birdsall, engineers have designed new joints that can more easily withstand the bending movements.

Changes great and small have been made in the Bridge throughout its history. When the Bridge first opened, it supported two lanes for cable cars and four lanes for horse-drawn vehicles. This was changed in 1898 to four lanes for mass transit and two for other vehicles. Growing automobile use after World War II led to complete removal of all tracks and the redesign of the truss carrying the roadway.

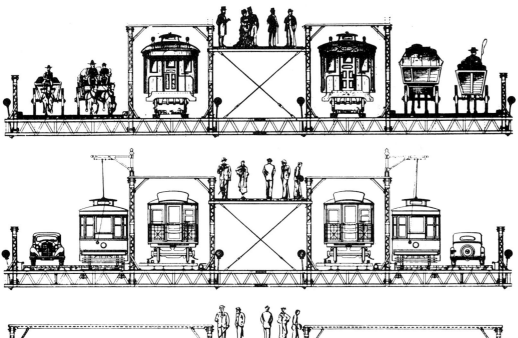

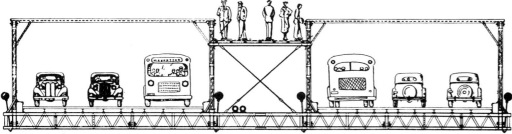

These drawings from a 1945 engineer's report illustrate the modifications that have been made in the Brooklyn Bridge's roadway. At top is a cross section of the roadway as it appeared in 1883. In 1898 (middle) two lanes for trolley cars were added. The change that was proposed in 1945 and made in 1952 (bottom) eliminated all the tracks and extended the overhead beams to the edge of the roadway.

Now the Bridge is evolving again, changing to better survive the rigors of New York City and better serve its population. City and state officials say the renovation of the Bridge will take at least fifteen years (see table below)

A fifteen-year renovation program for the Brooklyn Bridge was laid out by the New York State Department of Transportation after inspections in the late 1970s showed the extent of deterioration. The state thinks the actual timetable will extend well into the twenty-first century because not all funds will be available sooner.

Construction Date	Cost (millions)	Description
1980-81	2.2	Rebuild foundation protection around Brooklyn tower; replace old wood piers with soil-filled steel walls.
1981-82	5.0	Resurface promenade and rebuild access steps; add new ramps.
1983-84	20.0	Restore cable anchorages; replace cables that are too badly corroded to remain.
1986-87	26.0	Replace decks on approaches (between the towers and the anchorages); replace suspenders and diagonals; misc. work on main cables.
1990-91	25.0	Strengthen structure of bridge, particularly roadway truss.
1994-95	25.0	Rehabilitate and replace approach ramps (between anchorages and city streets); improve lighting; modify drainage system for easier maintenance.
TOTAL	103.2	
Plus engineering studies	2.2	
GRAND TOTAL	105.4	

The nineteen independent strands splay away from ring castings on the main cable as they enter the anchorage tunnels. After the cables are repaired, the castings may be moved a bit toward the river to allow more room between strands inside the anchorages.
Photo: Steven S. Ross

and maybe as long as thirty if funds continue to trickle in at the current slow rate.

Many of the changes will be almost imperceptible to the average citizen. Some will be obvious to just about everybody. Some have engendered either public controversy or technical debate. A few contemplated changes are as technically daring and innovative as the Bridge itself was a hundred years ago.

The Promenade

The most obvious change to users is the controversial alteration that was made in the promenade when a large section of it was replaced in 1982. There was little quarrel over the choice of plank materials—South American greenheart, one of the strongest, toughest woods known. The wood is so tough that nails cannot be driven into it. Holes are drilled in the planks, and they are fastened down with stainless steel screws.

The controversy centered instead around access to the promenade. Although it was originally meant for casual walking, it has long been open to bicycles. But cyclists have had to negotiate steep steps to use the Bridge. Now, with gradually sloping ramps added, some people fear the cyclists will eventually force pedestrians off the promenade entirely.

"The change is necessary," argued George Zaimes, chief engineer for the New York State Department of Transportation's New York City office. "People in wheelchairs will be able to use the promenade. And, more importantly, the ramps will allow the Bridge to be fully patrolled by police on scootercars."

Main Cables

The Brooklyn Bridge was built in an age when bridge collapses were common, and yet it was half again as large as any suspension bridge then standing. It is hardly surprising, then, that the Bridge's designers—John and Washington Roebling—were extremely cautious in their calculations. Each of the four main cables contains nineteen strands. Each of the strands, in turn, contains about 280 separate wires—each one a bit thinner than a pencil. Taken together, the cables are strong enough to support more than five times the weight of roadway and vehicles they actually have to.

Each of the nineteen strands in each cable was spun out over the river one loop of wire at a time—from the Brooklyn anchorage, across the towers, to the Manhattan anchorage, where the wire loop was secured to an iron "shoe." After each spool of wire was finished, the next would be spliced on.

From anchorage to anchorage, the nineteen strands are bundled into a single cable almost sixteen inches in diameter, meticulously wrapped with wire and covered with fabric. Cast-steel rings hold the cable in one bundle where it enters the anchorage tunnel and divides into nineteen strands again. "From casting to casting the cables are in beautiful shape," said Blair Birdsall, head of Steinman Boynton Gronquist & Birdsall. Only a little water has leaked into the cables over the years, and the zinc coating around the individual wires has protected them from corrosion.

That is not the case, however, where the cables divide into strands inside the anchorage, and where each strand is connected to an eyebar. There, the anchorages are cave-like tunnels of limestone. "We had trouble even getting inside to do the inspection," said George Zaimes. "In order to see all the wires where they go around the eyebar pins, we had to use fiber optics. No one had been able to see this area since it was built more than a hundred years ago."

The engineers were alarmed by what they saw. A hundred years of water dripping into this critical space had corroded many of the individual wires, and an earlier, misguided preservation effort had made things worse.

"Someone thought they would protect the eyebars and dumped concrete on top of them in some of the anchorage tunnels," said Zaimes. "The concrete is porous. It absorbed the water and held it right on the wires, greatly increasing the rate of corrosion."

Of the 152 strand-and-eyebar loops (nineteen at each end of each of the four main cables), at least two and as many as twenty will have to be replaced, starting in 1983. Such a task has never been attempted. Once a strand has been identified as needing to be repaired, a special clamp designed by the Steinman firm will be used to hold the strand tightly against the weight of the Bridge itself. The strand will then be cut through, each of its 280-odd wires cleaned of rust and dirt, and a steel socket pulled over the clean wires. The wires will be spread apart to form a cone-shaped brush within the socket, and the socket will be preheated to receive molten zinc.

Until engineers at Columbia University tested the technique on a full-size mockup of the anchorage, no cable of this size had ever been socketed in a horizontal position. "And it has never been done in so confined a space as the anchorage tunnels," said Dr. Maciej P. Bieniek, the Columbia civil engineering professor who helped direct the project.

The Columbia researchers heated the zinc until it was liquid, then poured it down a twelve-foot funnel and pipe to the socket assembly. This simulated what will actually take place: the zinc will be heated outside the anchorage tunnels, then piped to the new sockets. Inside the anchorages, the sockets will have to be kept heated to at least six hundred degrees Fahrenheit, so that the zinc flows evenly around all the wires in the strands without leaving voids or cracks.

The engineers considered using instead a dense plastic that can be poured as a liquid and allowed to harden in the sockets. The plastic would have removed the need to heat the whole assembly, and tests at Columbia and Lehigh University confirmed that it is more than strong enough to do the job. "But no installation using the plastic has been in service more than six or seven years," said Bieniek. "We didn't want to take a chance."

The engineers did not want to take a chance with the Bridge's vertical wire-rope suspenders, either. "Superficially they looked fine," said Birdsall. "But we thought we should take a closer look. Once we did, we found the molten metal used to form the sockets at the ends of the suspenders had not penetrated very far. The metal, probably lead, congealed at the big end of each socket." Only a little bit of metal is keeping each suspender from pulling loose.

While even this little bit seems enough—no suspender has ever failed—the engineers say the margin of safety is not too great. All the suspenders will be replaced. George Zaimes has suggested selling the old suspenders in short lengths as souvenirs. Some 500,000 pieces could be cut. At $50 each, Zaimes could raise $25 million to pay for more maintenance and repairs. The

View of wire-rope suspender cable showing socket of the type thought to be defective.
Photo: Steven S. Ross

Steinman engineer Janusz Kupiec inside the anchorage tunnel.
Photo: Steven S. Ross

same thing was done with wire rope from the Golden Gate Bridge's suspenders when they were replaced in the mid-1970s.

The diagonal stays will also be replaced. They are badly corroded in spots, especially at the tops of the towers, where they pass through in rather untidy tangles. The Steinman firm has designed a neater system to hold the diagonals in place and lessen the chance of rust and of chafing against the stone towers themselves.

The Roadway

Birdsall also wants to fix the "kinks" in the Bridge—three-foot humps in the roadway on both sides of each of the towers. "We can do it by adjusting the new suspenders and diagonals," he said.

Although the main cables and new suspension ropes and diagonals would be able to hold the weight of any modern vehicle, the roadway deck and the steel beams of the truss that supports the deck cannot. Taken together, the deck and the truss can carry a load only about half that of modern bridges. Because of that, and because the overhead beams of the truss leave only eleven feet of clearance, the Brooklyn Bridge will not be opened to truck traffic. The roadway is more than adequate for cars, however, and even for buses once the suspenders are replaced.

The engineers also see a time when the existing roadway deck, with its steel grid, could be replaced. Because the grid is slippery when wet, short studs were welded on to keep cars from weaving in bad weather. If a new deck system could be designed, the studs could be removed—and so could the loud whine they produce. That would make a walk on the promenade more pleasant than it is today.

The concrete approach ramps will need to be replaced in the 1990s. When that's done, their layout could be changed to accomodate the traffic needs of the time.

Other Concerns

Engineers and contractors working on the Bridge express continued amazement at the quality of materials and workmanship. Even the supposedly dangerous, brittle wire of J. Lloyd Haigh appears strong enough to last indefinitely, according to Columbia's Bieniek. But other problems will have to be corrected eventually if the Brooklyn Bridge is ever to rival the lifespan of, say, Europe's great cathedrals.

The anchorages rest on underground grillworks of criss-crossed wood timbers, which allow the anchorage stones to settle evenly without cracking. The timbers are in perfect shape on the Manhattan side, but in Brooklyn the

When the deck was rebuilt in 1952, concrete was poured into a light but strong steel grid. The big drawback: the studs, added to keep cars from slipping on the grid in wet weather, cause much noise and wear the tires of vehicles using the Bridge.
Photo: Steven S. Ross

level of ground water has receded, leaving them dry. They will eventually rot unless the water table can be raised permanently, or unless some new technology is invented to preserve them.

Where the main cables pass over the towers, they rest on great cast-iron "saddles," each thirteen feet long and four feet wide. In modern suspension bridges, the saddles can easily move a foot or so to release stresses as the structure expands or contracts, or reacts to unusual winds or heavy loads. The saddles on the Brooklyn Bridge have rollers, too, but the rollers are small, and records show the saddles have moved very little since the Bridge was opened for traffic in 1883. As a result, stresses have bent a few steel beams in the truss carrying the roadway. The bends are barely perceptible—in fact, some have existed since at least 1898—but they are a warning that the design is not perfect.

Until now, the engineers believed the rollers were simply poorly designed, and that their small size allowed rust to immobilize them. During research undertaken for the present renovation, however, Steinman engineers found statements made by the Bridge's builders to the effect that the rollers were meant to function only while the Bridge was under construction. Any major modification or renovation of the Bridge's basic structure would have to take this into account.

Washington Roebling also designed a cable system under the roadway truss that was supposed to help keep the Bridge from swaying. The Bridge doesn't sway much anyway, so some of the cables don't have to be there. "The so-called parabolic cables are of little use, and since they are a maintenance problem, they may be removed," said Janusz Kupiec, a Steinman engineer who has been studying the structure since 1980.

The engineers also worry a bit about the roadway truss itself, since no joint between the beams of the truss has ever been taken apart for a close look. Computer analysis shows that the truss beams are thicker and stronger than they have to be. But even though some corrosion would thus be acceptable, a typical joint will be dismantled to make sure corrosion has not reached the danger point.

The Future

These worries are all minor ones. The engineers say that the Brooklyn Bridge could last as long as the city it serves—and maybe longer. It will last, that is, if the city's citizens and political leaders invest in its upkeep.

That investment should be forthcoming as long as everyone realizes that the ravages of the past thirty years of "deferred maintenance" are lessons we cannot afford to repeat.

Parabolic cables cross under the maintenance walkway at midspan.
Photo: Steven S. Ross

177

Selected Filmography

Charles Reichenthal

For decades, motion pictures have greatly underscored the Brooklyn Bridge's image as the definitive symbol of New York City by utilizing the venerable span as the ultimate signature of the Big Apple. Scores of films—from super epics to B movies—have focused in on the Bridge for opening shots, thus immediately establishing location of the film and, perhaps, the very mood of the work itself. Sometimes, the Bridge has been part of a brilliant tableau of the city, as in *West Side Story*. At other times, it has served as another sort of symbol, as in *Saturday Night Fever*, where an automobile ride across the Bridge indicates John Travolta's growth from "small town hero" to "big city hopeful." The Bridge has turned up in such varied works as *Cover Girl, King Kong, No Way to Treat a Lady, The Detective, The Beast from 20,000 Fathoms, The Kid from Brooklyn, The Sentinel, Sweet November, Youngblood Hawk, Loving, A Fine Madness, Superman, Escape from New York, Park Row, City Across the River*, and so on *ad infinitum*. The following is a representative sampling of films that have used the setting of the Bridge for narrative and other cinematic purposes.

The Bowery 1931. *Director: Raoul Walsh*
Wallace Beery, George Raft, Jackie Cooper, and Fay Wray. The fast-moving story of Steve Brodie (played by Raft), who, New York mythology insists, jumped from the Brooklyn Bridge on a bet.

Every Day's a Holiday 1938. *Director: A. Edward Sutherland*
Classic comedy starring Mae West, Edmund Lowe, Charles Butterworth, Louis Armstrong, and Lloyd Nolan. The unsinkable Ms. West is told to leave New York after she is involved in a continuing "scam" to sell the Brooklyn Bridge to unsuspecting men. One scene on the Bridge (Hollywood variety) shows the ploys with which the Brooklyn-born Mae accomplishes her "sale."

Force of Evil 1948. *Director: Abraham Polonsky*
John Garfield, Beatrice Pearson, Marie Windsor, and Thomas Gomez. A true "cult" film—generally considered to be one of the best of the forties films that tried to analyze crime and the syndicate. The climax takes place in the shadow of the Bridge at the site of the current Empire-Fulton Ferry State Park.

Godspell 1973. *Director: David Greene*
The classy film version of the Broadway/off-Broadway stage hit with theater star Victor Garber (*Little Me, Sweeney Todd*) in the pivotal role. The film opens with Garber singing his way across the Bridge in a beautiful on-location scene.

Guilty Bystander 1950. *Director: Joseph Lerner*
Zachary Scott, Faye Emerson, and Mary Boland. A neglected film. An intense drama about a kidnapping. This dark, brooding work utilizes a finale that takes place on and around the area that now sports the River Café, Ferrybank Restaurant, and Musicbarge. Comedienne Boland here performs a malevolent role with brilliance.

It Happened in Brooklyn 1947. *Director: Richard Whorf*
An enjoyable, though smaller-scale MGM musical of the forties, starring such MGM regulars as Frank Sinatra, Kathryn Grayson, Peter Lawford, Jimmy Durante, and Gloria Grahame. Sinatra sings the song "Brooklyn Bridge" in this story involving Brooklynites trying to "make it" in show biz. The song is performed on the Bridge itself.

Marathon Man 1976. *Director: John Schlesinger*
One of the most exciting spy-chase thrillers of the seventies, starring Dustin Hoffman, Sir Laurence Olivier, and Roy Scheider. In one of the nail-biting sequences, Hoffman, on foot, tries to elude a group of neo-Nazis who are chasing him across the Bridge.

'Neath Brooklyn Bridge 1942. *Director: Wallace Fox*
Vintage Grade-B film featuring the group that made up, at various times, the Bowery Boys, the Dead End Kids, and the East Side Kids—Leo Gorcey, Huntz Hall, Bobby Jordan, and Gabriel Dell. By the time this Monogram film was made, the Dead End Kids had mellowed; the once-vicious juvenile delinquents of the original "Dead End" had become comic, "Brooklynese-talking," street-wise do-gooders.

On the Town 1949. *Directors: Stanley Donen and Gene Kelly*
One of MGM's groundbreaking musicals, starring Gene Kelly, Frank Sinatra, Vera-Ellen, Betty Garrett, Ann Miller, Jules Munshin, and Alice Pearce. This classic version of the Leonard Bernstein-Betty Comden-Adolph Green musical has early scenes of sailors leaving the Navy Yard to cross the Bridge and spend shore leaves in Manhattan (they wind up in a Hollywood-studio Coney Island).

Saboteur 1942. *Director: Alfred Hitchcock*
Robert Cummings, Priscilla Lane, and Otto Kruger. One of Hitchcock's thrilling spy-chase adventures in which hero Cummings (mistakenly thought to be a murderous arsonist) tracks down the true culprits by following the Nazi agents across the entire country. In one chilling scene, the villains sink a ship in New York harbor. Characters see the ship (actually the *Normandie*) overturned below them as they drive across the Brooklyn Bridge.

Sophie's Choice 1982. *Director: Alan J. Pakula*
Critically acclaimed version of the William Styron novel. Meryl Streep stars in one of the most lauded performances of the decade. Kevin Kline and Peter MacNicol play the two men in Sophie's powerful story. Scenes shot in Flatbush, Prospect Park, and on the Bridge.

Tarzan's New York Adventure 1942. *Director: Richard Thorpe*
Johnny Weissmuller, Maureen O'Sullivan, Johnny Sheffield, Charles Bickford, and Paul Kelly. A strong entry in the early MGM Tarzan series. Tarzan—manipulated by the plot to visit New York—takes a dive off the Bridge.

A View from the Bridge 1962. *Director: Sidney Lumet*
Raf Vallone, Carol Lawrence, Jean Sorel, Maureen Stapleton, and Raymond Pellegrin. Powerful version of the Arthur Miller play. One of many films that Lumet has set in New York City (often with the assistance of the Brooklyn Bridge).

Winterset 1936. *Director: Alfred Santell*
The highly praised film version of the Maxwell Anderson prize-winning play. A poignant melodrama that takes place in the shadow of the Bridge, although this stage-bound version was filmed entirely in a movie studio. The cast includes Burgess Meredith, Margo, John Carradine, and Edward Ellis.

The Wiz 1978. *Director: Sidney Lumet*
Diana Ross (as modern-day Dorothy), Michael Jackson, and Lena Horne. Splashy version of the Broadway super hit, with scenes all over New York City, including most notably the Bridge, all gussied up for the occasion. Another one of Lumet's New York-based films.

Wolfen 1980. *Director: Michael Wadleigh*
Albert Finney in a spine-chilling yarn about werewolf-like beasts on the loose in New York City. Spectacular special effects are employed as the "beast" makes its way across the Brooklyn Bridge at night.

Two independently made non-commercial films not to be overlooked are the 1921 avant-garde classic **Mannahatta** (produced, directed, and filmed by Paul Strand and Charles Sheeler) and the delightful 1981 documentary **Brooklyn Bridge** (produced and directed by Ken Burns). The Burns film garnered an Academy award nomination in the documentary category.

One major Broadway play has utilized part of the Brooklyn Bridge saga for its plot. A musical called *Kelly*, it was a one-performance flop of 1965. Lavishly produced by a powerhouse group composed of David Susskind and Daniel Melnick in association with Joseph E. Levine, it was based on the story of Steve Brodie (see film *The Bowery*), who purportedly leaped from the Bridge in order to win a bet. Although it was a smash hit on the road, it failed to attain any acceptance in New York.

Selected Bibliography

1   Robert Greenhaigh Albion, *The Rise of The New York Port 1815–1860* (New York: Charles Scribner's Sons, 1939).

2   Charles Barnard, "The Brooklyn Bridge," *St. Nicholas Magazine* (July 1883).

3   A. C. Barnes, *The New York and Brooklyn Bridge,* pamphlet (Brooklyn, 1883).

4   Archibald Black, *The Story of Bridges* (New York: McGraw-Hill, 1936).

5   B. A. Botkin, *New York City Folk Lore* (New York: Random House, 1956).

6   Francis Williams Brown, *Big Bridge to Brooklyn* (New York: Aladdin Books, 1956).

7   James H. Callendar, *Yesterdays on Brooklyn Heights* (Brooklyn: The Dorland Press, 1927).

8   *East River Bridge: Laws and Engineers Reports, 1868–1884* (Brooklyn: Brooklyn Eagle Press, 1885).

9   Edward Robb Ellis, *The Epic of New York City* (New York: Coward-McCann, 1966).

10   E. F. Farrington, *Concise Description of the East River Bridge, with Full Details of the Construction,* pamphlet (New York: C. D. Wynkoop, 1881; republished Brooklyn: Boro Book Store, 1969).

11   S. W. Green, *A Complete History of the New York and Brooklyn Bridge: From Its Conception in 1866 to Its Completion in 1883,* pamphlet (New York: 1883).

12   H. J. Hopkins, *A Span of Bridges: An Illustrated History* (New York: Praeger, 1970).

13   Henry W. B. Howard, *History of the City of Brooklyn* (Brooklyn: The Brooklyn Eagle Press, 1893).

14   David Jacobs and Anthony E. Neville, *Bridges, Canals & Tunnels: The Engineering Conquest of America* (New York: American Heritage Publishing in association with The Smithsonian, 1968).

15   John A. Kouwenhoven, *The Columbia Historical Portrait of New York* (New York: Doubleday and Company, 1953).

16   David McCullough, *The Great Bridge* (New York: Simon and Schuster, 1972).

17   David McCullough, "The Treasure from the Carpentry Shop: The Extraordinary Original Drawings of the Brooklyn Bridge," *American Heritage* 31, no. 1 (December 1979).

18   Sharon Reier, *The Bridges of New York* (New York: Quadrant Press, 1977).

19   Hamilton Schuyler, *The Roeblings: A Century of Engineers, Bridge Builders, and Industrialists: The Story of Three Generations of an Illustrious Family, 1831–1931* (New Jersey: Princeton University Press, 1931).

20   Montgomery Schuyler, "Brooklyn Bridge as a Monument," *Harper's Weekly* (May 26, 1883); reprinted in *Roots of Contemporary American Architecture,* ed. Lewis Mumford (New York: Grove Press, 1959).

21   Montgomery Schuyler, *American Architecture and Other Writings,* ed. William H. Jody and Ralph Coe (Cambridge: Belknap Press, 1961).

22   David B. Steinman, *The Builders of the Bridge: The Story of John Roebling and His Sons* (New York: Harcourt Brace & Co., 1945).

23   David B. Steinman, *Bridges and Their Builders* (New York: G. P. Putnam's Sons, 1945).

24   Henry R. Stiles, *The Civil, Political, Professional and Ecclesiastical History and Commercial and Industrial Record of the County of Kings and the City of Brooklyn, N.Y., from 1683 to 1884* (New York: Munsell and Co., 1884).

25   Isaac Newton Phelps Stokes, *The Iconography of Manhattan Island 1498-1909 Compiled from Original Sources and Illustrated by Photointaglio Reproductions of Important Maps, Plans, Views and Documents in Public and Private Collections,* 6 volumes (New York: Robert H. Dodd, 1915–1918).

26   Alan Trachtenberg, *Brooklyn Bridge, Fact and Symbol* (New York: Oxford University Press, 1965).

27   Archibald Douglas Turnbull, *John Stevens, An American Record* (New York: Century Co., 1928).

28   Norval White and Elliot Willensky, *American Institute of Architecture Guide to New York City* (New York: The Macmillan Co., 1968; Collier Books, 1978).